JERUSALEM
reflection of eternity

For Barbara
with love
Eliane

June 1998

JERUSALEM
reflection of eternity

ELIANE WILSON   MOTKE BLUM

Shepheard-Walwyn (Publishers) Ltd

First published in 1990 by
Shepheard-Walwyn (Publishers) Ltd
26 Charing Cross Road (Suite 34)
LONDON WC2H 0DH

ISBN 0 85683 113 1

Jacket design by Mietek Orbach
Page layout by Frederick Marns
Photography by Shuki Kook
Typesetting by Alacrity Phototypesetters
Banwell Castle, Weston-super-Mare, Avon
Colour separation by ArtPlus, Jerusalem
Printed and bound in Italy by
A. Mondadori Editore, Verona

Contents

To Peace

Let us be like the lines that lead to the centre of a circle
uniting there
and not like parallel lines which never meet

Countless works of art and literature have been dedicated to Jerusalem in the course of generations. Many of these have been devoted to Jerusalem as a symbol, an idea, a dream. But beside the heavenly city, there are many other Jerusalems.

There is Jerusalem in the depth of time, the historic city, the eternal capital of the Jewish people.

There is Jerusalem of the great faiths with their common roots and differences.

Over and above these and side by side with them, there is the living, breathing and beautiful Jerusalem.

And within are concentrated many conflicts and challenges with which we are coping with patience and tolerance, while looking to the future with sensitivity and preservation of the heritage of the past. Despite all the difficulties, we will continue our efforts to ensure the future of Jerusalem as the 'City of Peace'.

This impressive book, edited with great love and devotion by Eliane Wilson, and intertwined with the paintings of the Jerusalem artist Motke Blum, gives expression to the wealth and the diversity of the literature, the thoughts and the prayers written about Jerusalem.

Teddy Kollek

Preface

To Jerusalem my city I wanted to say aloud
words that I whisper to her heart
so my ears too would hear what my heart feels
                                    *

To catch all the strands of the web still floating in a straight
line in the air and to make them one again

so that a heart beat would pulse from one end to the other
                                                    in endless

perfect frequency

and the circuit would renew itself forever humming my speech
with all the words I know and don't know

beyond all the tongues I've seen in the mirror in rainbow colors
from bottom to top

and more
                                    *

I knew in the dream the dream wouldn't fly like a dream.
I knew in the dream that in me myriads are dreaming
                                                    the dream.
I woke. Midnight. Who turns the dark of night into the
                                                    light of day?
The sun stands still in the window in the dream as on that day
                                                    in Gibeon I recall.
Look, here comes the night that is day and not night
and the endless day comes in the midst of night. And it will
                                                    never darken.
And morning light glows. I wake. Look, here before me,
                                                    Jerusalem.
And I see it. I see it with myriads of eyes.
Was there ever anything like this
a dream dreamed at the same time
by myriads while they dream.
                                                    Amir Gilboa

There is a story told by the sages and handed down from age to age that when God had finished making the world, He asked one of the angels if anything was wanting on land or sea, in air or heaven. The angel replied that nearly all was perfect; one thing only was lacking: speech with which to praise God's work. God approved the angel's words and, mingling dust from the four corners of the earth, He fashioned man and woman and breathed a soul into them.

And man sang. With love and fierce devotion, he sang the city whose sound is unlike any other sound in the history of mankind — the city of Mount Moriah where lies the Foundation Stone set by God as a blessing to the world. On the mountain of myrrh and frankincense, Abraham offered Isaac; and Jacob in a dream saw a ladder reaching to heaven. The Ten Commandments given to Moses and to each one of us, were hewn from the Rock on which, in another time, the Prophet Muhammad would leave the imprint of his heel when ascending to heaven on his Night Journey. With the Song of Songs in his heart, man sang the city whose name embodies his longing for union with the divine: *Yerushalaym*, eternal meeting between heaven and earth. *Urbs Jerusalem beata*, City of God, city of men. *Al-Quds*, the Holy.

This book started many years ago as a personal journey. One day, on a visit to Jerusalem after a very long absence, I entered the studio of Motke Blum. Reflected in his paintings were the thousands of words I had read about the city. I recounted to him 'The Legend of the Third Dove' and as I spoke, Stefan Zweig's story of the lost and mystical dove fluttering between heaven and earth in her search for peace, became the invisible thread tying together poetry, prose and canvas. 'I am a harp for your songs', wrote Judah ha-Levi, the poet of the Spanish Hebrew Golden Age. I hope the pages of this book will echo his words.

The origins of Jerusalem are rooted deep in the antiquity of the land of Canaan. Meeting place between continents and civilizations, this is the land of the Promise, the land into which God leads Israel to join them to each other in a mysterious and everlasting bond.

Jerusalem lies on the edge of the Judean desert, where, at the beginning of the third millenium B.C.E. (Before the Christian Era), an Early Bronze Age settlement was established close to the waters of the Gihon Spring where Solomon would be annointed king, and Jesus would send a blind man to wash his eyes and who came back seeing.

When the might of Assyria came against Jerusalem, King Hezekiah had a tunnel bored through the rock to bring the waters of the Gihon inside the city, into the Pool of Siloam. And because its waters flow from the Garden of Eden, soothing the pain of sorrows of those who drink from it, the Arabs call it *Ain-Silwan*, the Spring of Consolation.

It is in the Egyptian Execration Texts from the 19th Century B.C.E. that the name of *Urushamem* is recorded for the first time and sometime between the end of the Bronze and the beginning of the Iron Age, appears the King-Priest Melchizedek who, with bread and wine, greets Abram, Father of all believers.

The story of Jerusalem — city of Peace — begins three thousand years ago when Jebus, the stronghold held by the Jebusites, fell to the shepherd, annointed King, David. Warrior, statesman, and Psalmist of Israel, David not only made the citadel city the capital of his kingdom and the site of the royal fort, but also the sanctuary which housed the Ark of the Law. 'O how I love thy Law. It has been to me not a burden but a song', sang David who danced before the Lord as the Ark was brought with rejoicing to the City of David. Thus Jerusalem became the religious centre of Israel — its love and faith bound for all time with the city of God, Zion, 'the city of the Great King'. From there Judaism, mother-faith to Christianity and Islam, would bequeath to mankind the concept of ethical monotheism and the rule of moral law, the law that fulfils itself as a law of love and justice.

Later, between the 8th and the 5th centuries, B.C.E., the divinely inspired voice of the Prophets was heard, soaring amidst 'the rushing of nations that rush like the rushing of mighty waters' — Assyria, Babylonia, and Persia. These prophets proclaimed the unity of morality and religion. They chastised the people for their indifference, denounced injustice and oppression, and demanded social justice — but always compassionate, they comforted Israel in its wanderings and exiles, and foresaw the return when God would gather its people from the east and the west, from the north and the south, bringing them home to Jerusalem. And rising beyond the boundaries of the Hebrew nation, to encompass all humanity, they spoke of the sanctity of life, mercy and peace, 'when nation shall not take up sword against nation and they shall never again know war'.

In the 3rd century B.C.E. the Macedonian conqueror Alexander the Great, established his realm on the ruins of the Persian Empire. An historic legend, told by Josephus, describes Alexander's visit to Jerusalem, when he confirmed the Jews' right to live according to their ancestral Law; but Alexander had a vision of cultural fusion between the East and West through the dissemination of the Greek civilization. In Egypt, the city of Alexandria became the established centre of Hellenism. 'Seek not to understand what is too wonderful for thee', wrote Joshua Ben Sira in his book of *Wisdom* — a book which his grandson translated into Greek in the 2nd century B.C.E. and which the Old Latin Bible would call *Ecclesiasticus*. Centre of the largest Jewish community in the diaspora, it was in Alexandria too that the Bible was translated for the first time and, in an attempt to bridge the gulf between Greeks and Jews, *The Letter of Aristeas* describes the translation of the Hebrew Pentateuch into Greek, the *Septuagint*, by the seventy-two elders sent from Jerusalem.

However, it was not the Hellenism of classical Greece imbued with the spirit of her philosophers which reached Judea, and to which many Jews were attracted, but a decadent and debased Hellenism, tearing at the fabric of moral and religious life. When the Seleucid King, Antiochus IV, who had conferred on himself the title of 'Theos Epiphanus' (the evident god), defiled the Temple and, under pain of death forbade the observance of the ancestral religion, rebellion flared. Judas, called 'Maccabeus' (the Hammer), liberated the city and on the 25th December in the year 165 B.C.E., to the music of harps, lutes and cymbals, and the rekindling of the seven-branched candelabrum, the Menorah, he re-dedicated the Temple. The undefiled oil, sufficient for one night only, according to the Jewish legend, lasted eight days.

Some hundred years later, Pompey captured Jerusalem and Judea became a Roman province. In his *Jewish War*, Josephus Flavius describes the magnificence of Jerusalem during the reign of King Herod.

Then in A.D. 70, after a siege of inconceivable horror and slaughter, the city fell to Titus. It was the ninth of the Hebrew month of Ab. Six-hundred and fifty-seven years earlier, in that very month, on that very day, the Babylonians had set ablaze Solomon's Temple. Now Jerusalem's second Temple was in flames, the city sacked and razed to the ground, her people taken into captivity: *Judea capta est*. On the site of the ruined Temple, the Emperor Hadrian erected a temple to his god Jupiter and, after quelling Judea's last desperate and heroic attempt for freedom, the Bar-Kokhba revolt in A.D. 135, he built a new Roman city called Aelia Capitolina. The name Judea was expunged, replaced by Palestine, and the Jews were forbidden to enter their holy city. Two centuries later, they would be allowed, once a year, on the anniversary of the destruction of the Temple, to come and pray at the Western Wall, all that was left standing of the Temple — but from which the divine Presence, the Shekhina, would never depart.

Although estranged from its land, to which it would return nineteen centuries later, Israel, through its spiritual and cultural life, retained its national consciousness. When in 444 B.C.E., whilst Nehemia was governor of Judea, Ezra the Scribe re-taught the Torah to the Jews recently returned from the exile in Babylonia, he was passing on to future generations a spiritual heritage from which they would draw an indomitable strength, that, uniting and guiding them, ensured their survival. And through all the tears of the exile, in its poetry, prayer and liturgical music, Israel would sing Jerusalem. *Yerushalaym shel mata*, earthly Jerusalem twinned with *Yerushaiaym shel ma'ala*, Jerusalem the heavenly. The City of memories and expectations. The city of eternal hope.

In the Armenian Orthodox Chapel of the Holy Sepulchre, one can still see today, etched under an ancient drawing of a boat, the words *Domine Ivimus* 'Lord we came', written by an early pilgrim, on the stones of the holiest of all Christian sites. With the conversion of the Emperor Constantine in the 4th century A.D. Christianity had become the official faith of the Roman Empire; its province of Palestine a Christian Holy Land. The emperor's mother, the Empress Helena, journeyed to Jerusalem to worship at the places which had witnessed the last days of Jesus, and these she sanctified by erecting numerous shrines. In the 5th century, the Church Father Jerome wrote: 'Just as those who have seen Athens understand Greek history better, and just as those who have seen Troy understand the words of the poet Virgil, thus one will comprehend the Holy Scriptures with a clearer understanding who has seen the land of Judah with his own eyes ...'

Like many Jews accused of sedition, Jesus, the gentle Teacher of the Law and the Prophets, had been nailed to a Roman cross. For his disciples, he was the Innocent Lamb who had offered himself in expiation for the sins of all mankind. And to Hierusalem, hallowed by the Passion of their Saviour, Christian pilgrims from all over the Roman Empire came to pray and touch the holy relics in the newly-erected chapels, oratories and churches, and to walk in Jesus' steps. Across the Kidron Valley, they climbed the Mount of Olives to the Garden of Gethsemane, *Gat Shemanim* (the oil press) where Jesus kneeled down and prayed that the cup, if it were possible, might be removed from him; and among the olive trees, Mary, his mother, was buried.

In the 6th century, the Emperor Justinian, dedicated

13

to the Virgin Mary a magnificent 'New Church'. Last imperial benefactor to Christian Jerusalem before the crusades, Justinian also built hospices and a hospital for nursing pilgrims.

After a short-lived occupation by the Persians in the 7th century, Jerusalem returned to Byzantine rule. By then the Muslims were marching towards Palestine and Islam came to Jerusalem when Caliph Omar, in A.D. 638, entered the Holy City. That was six years after the death of the Prophet Muhammad, who had proclaimed the Unity and the Oneness of Allah.

'In the Name of God, the Compassionate, the Merciful', Omar guaranteed to Christian inhabitants their lives, churches and property and permitted the Jews, the People of the Book, to return to the city. 'Glory be to Him who carried His Servant by night from the Sacred Mosque to the Farthest Mosque' reads the Holy Qur'an. The Temple Esplanade became the *Haram esh-Sherif*, the Noble Sanctuary; Jerusalem, *al-Quds*, the Holy, third holy place in Islam after Mecca, the Prophet's birthplace, and Medina, to which he had made his *hijira* accompanied by his faithful.

For four hundred years, from its distant capitals, Islam ruled Jerusalem. Dynasties came and went: the *Umayyads*, who bequeathed Jerusalem one of the jewels of Islam, the Dome of the Rock; the *Abbasids*, of whom history remembers the monarch Harun al-Rashid, whose friendship with the Holy Roman Emperor Charlemagne, was cemented by frequent embassies and exchanges of gifts. To Jerusalem — which he had endowed with a hospice, church and convent for Latin pilgrims — medieval chroniclers, in their writings, brought Charlemagne to Jerusalem, and the Caliph offered him the keys of the Holy Sepulchre. Later came the Egyptian *Fatimids* who

reconstructed the *El-Aksa* Mosque after the earthquake which struck the city in 1033 and finally the *Seljuk* Turks, founders of the Turkish Empire.

Then in the name of Jerusalem and the vow to deliver the Holy Sepulchre from the Muslims, Europe launched the First Crusade. In the summer of 1099, the Crusaders stormed Jerusalem and put her population to the sword. The Latin Cross replaced the Crescent, crusaders' banners were flown over the battlements: the Latin Kingdom of Jerusalem was born. History records the name of its princes and knights endowed by romance with all the attributes of chivalry — Godfrey of Bouillon, Tancred, Baldwin, the first king of the Crusaders' kingdom, and Richard Coeur de Lion. But less than a century later, the forces of Salah ad Din had reconquered Jerusalem. He granted clemency to the Christians, and the Jews, barred from living there by the Crusaders, were once more allowed to settle in Jerusalem; later in the 13th century, a Jewish community was established which would exist uninterrupted until 1948.

In the History of the Holy City, completed in 1496, Mujir al-Din, a native of Jerusalem, describes the city ruled for over 250 years by the Mamelukes, great builders, patrons of the arts and founders of many learned institutions.

In 1516, Jerusalem underwent yet another change of sovereignty. For the next four centuries, she was ruled from Constantinople. The sultan Suleiman the Magnificent restored her ramparts, building the walls which surround her today, repaired her aqueducts and adorned her with many fountains. But after his reign for the next three centuries, Jerusalem was ruled by despotic governors and fell into neglect. 'To see its destroyed walls, its debris-filled moat, its city circuit choked with ruins, you would scarcely recognize this famous metropolis which once fought against the most powerful empires in the world ... you would scarcely recognize Jerusalem', wrote the Comte de Volney in 1784; feelings echoed by the French writer René de Chateaubriand, a quarter of a century later.

Ottoman rule came to an end in December 1917 when the city fell to the British commander, General Edmund Allenby. Some weeks earlier, the British Government, on the initiative of Chaim Weizmann, the future first President of the State of Israel, had issued the Balfour Declaration, recognizing the concept of a Jewish nation in its ancestral land.

'If you but will it,' it need not be a dream', Theodor Herzl had proclaimed half a century before the establishment of the Jewish state. Fired by his vision, thousands of Jews journeyed to fulfil the prophecy of Amos: 'they shall rebuild ruined cities and inhabit them; they shall plant vineyards and drink the wines; they shall till gardens and eat their fruits'.

'Oh tongue of my muse, thou Hebrew of old, we are one in the blood, indivisible twin' the poet David Shimoni sang, as the Hebrew language, revived and enriched by the unrelenting passion of Eliezer Ben Yehuda, became the everyday language. The Hebrew University of Jerusalem was inaugurated in 1925 on Mount Scopus, whilst religious and governmental institutions of the state in-the-making were also established.

'It is not enough for us to play a part as individuals in the cultural development of the human race', wrote Albert Einstein, 'we must also attempt tasks which only nations as a whole can perform. Palestine is not merely a place of refuge ... but the embodiment of the re-awakening of the corporate spirit of the entire Jewish nation'.

During the thirty years of the British Mandate, Christian churches and hospices were erected. Among them, not far from Moses Montefiore's Yemin Moshe and its windmill, the church of St. Andrew's holds dear the memory of Scotland's gallant king, Robert the Bruce, whose wish had been that his heart should be buried in the Holy City; and nearby, dedicated by Lord Allenby in 1933 as a meeting place where religious and political differences can be forgotten, rose the YMCA, living monument to the promotion of peace.

On the 14th May 1948, David Ben-Gurion proclaimed the establishment of the State of Israel — the resurrection of a nation after two thousand years — which in its first decade would see the ingathering of a million exiles from dozens of lands, survivors of the Holocaust, and from the ancient communities of the Middle East and North Africa. Within a few hours of its Declaration of Independence, the new State was attacked by six neighbouring Arab armies; they were held and pushed back, but Jerusalem, torn by an Armistice line, became a divided city. She would remain so for the next nineteen years when, following the Six Day War in 1967, she was reunified.

To the Western Wall, the Jewish people came to pray at the end of the longest march in history. And with them, the memory of six million Jews annihilated in the Holocaust. They are forever remembered in the Memorial of *Yad Vashem*, 'I will give in my house and within my walls a place and a name'. Honoured with them are the 'Righteous Gentiles' who, risking their own lives, saved Jews from death, fulfilling the Talmudic precept that whoever saves a life, saves the whole of creation.

In modern Jerusalem, whose heritage and beauty are lovingly preserved and cultivated, one can hear her call — the sound of the shofar, the alleluiah of her bells, the voice of the muezzin — all exalting the words of the Psalmist 'Every man was born there, all my Springs are in thee'. But the Gate of Mercy, the Golden Gate, is yet to open. And the lost and mystical dove of Stefan Zweig still flutters with weary wings, frightened, between heaven and earth in her search for peace, waiting for a hand to be put forth. Some hands are reaching out — especially the hand of Teddy Kollek, her Mayor who presided over reunification and who, ever since, has been striving to foster tolerance and understanding between the diverse communities living side by side in their multiplicity of faiths and ideologies.

City of the living and home to generations of citizens of the spirit, man comes to her as a pilgrim, bringing his dream, his vision, his prayer: *Jerusalem, where peace is established in the human heart between man and man, and from there goes out into the world. Jerusalem — where Man meets God in Love ...*

ELIANE WILSON
Harrow on the Hill and Jerusalem
Spring 1990

Acknowledgements

Vous revenez d'un de ces longs voyages ...
Vous avez pris des lieux et laissé de vous-même
Quelque chose en passant

Victor Hugo

Early that morning I climbed the Mount of Olives. I could hear the silence. In the distance, Jerusalem — suffused with a beauty that almost hurts. I had finished my book. Jerusalem has given me much. I would like to record my thanks to:

Teddy Kollek builder of bridges, to whom I dedicate the spirit of the Third Dove

Père Marcel Dubois who not only contributed the introduction to 'Urbs Jerusalem Beata', but also generously gave his time and introduced me to the luminous poetry of Sister Marie-Madeleine

Raphael Davara whose generous aid and advice I have enjoyed, and for sharing with me his love for Jerusalem and her beauty

Roger Tavor who selflessly contributed to the book, for his constant support, encouragement and friendship

Lova Eliav for his kindness in looking at the manuscript and his warm words of encouragement

Robert Friend for his rare friendship, and who enriched my knowledge of Hebrew poetry through his inspired translations. Here is one of his own poems, a poem dedicated to the memory of Leah Goldberg, one of Israel's most beloved poets.

It is a warm voice after all
that she hears calling
in the chill of a thin snow falling:

'Let go. Let go.
How easy to let go
and find a bed in the snow.

Time is an ill,
and ill
Let my arms hold you

as you drift beyond pain
beyond crying,
into my dreamless forever.'

Though she knows
the voice is kind
but lying,

though she knows
that everywhere is nowhere
under the snow,

she lets her last dream flow
into the skull
of repose,

lulled by that lover
who gathers her single rose.

Père Bruno Hussar whose credo 'never to break anything which carries life itself; to love, because to love is to live, and to give life', has led him to the creation of *Nevé Shalom/Wahat-as-Salam* — 'the Oasis of Peace'. Sharing in this belief that only through the meeting of men, can one find the true way to peace, Jews, Arabs and Christians have come to live together, the mad dream of this Israeli Priest, Nobel Peace Prize nominee. The small village of *Nevé Shalom* has become the site of a School for Peace where thousands of men and women have come, and are coming, to build bridges of trust, respect, mutual comprehension, and friendship. I will always treasure the warmth of his welcome whenever I come to Jerusalem.

Anne Le Meignien, Père Bruno's *ouvrière de la première heure et des heures suivantes* — dear Anne whom I shall always picture meeting in the peaceful loveliness of the garden of Isaiah House.

David Dean, the Director of the YMCA, where I spent many hours, and Yossi Eisenberg, offered me at all times their kind hospitality. I remember the voices, Hebrew and Arabic, of the children coming from the YMCA kindergarten. 'Our hope for peace' David Dean calls them.

I would also like to express my appreciation to Menachem Levine who kindly offered me the resources of the Archives of the Municipality of Jerusalem, Rabbi Tovia Ben Chochin and Dr. Shalom Ben Chochin who helped me with scholarly advice, Zev Birger who warmly encouraged me throughout my endeavour, Mietek Orbach for his expert assistance in the early stages of the book production.

My gratitude to The Jerusalem Foundation and The Friends of the University of Jerusalem.

My thanks also to Judy Cohen, Winston Doul, Charles Janiv and Mounder Shama, for their help and friendliness.

The Studio of Shuki Kook photographed Motke Blum's original paintings, and Tzvika Yohanan and Chaim Gross at ArtPlus did the colour separations. The quality of their work was matched and surpassed only by their dedication to the whole project.

Shirley and Hillel Daleski offered me their gracious and warm hospitality on my frequent visits to Jerusalem. I shall not forget Dr. Subhi Abu-Gosh who introduced me to a lifelong addiction to coffee with cardamon ...

Rosa Beja, une amie d'enfance — pour son amitié

To Shoshana Blum, wife of the artist, who helped with the book in every sort of way and always made me welcome in her home, my deep affection.

For permission to include their poems, my thanks to: Yehuda Amichai, 'If I Forget Thee, Jerusalem' and 'The Windmill in Yemin Moshe'; Raphael Davara, 'A Song of Ascents'; Hadassah Haskale, 'Holy Sepulchre' (Seven Gates); Nidaa Khouri, 'Isaac'; Nathan Yonatan, 'Jerusalem' — and for his gracious welcome; Inna Pommeranz for 'My City' by Miriam Tal.

For generously giving me permission to use their translations of the following poems of which they hold the copyright, my thanks to: Robert Friend for 'Jerusalem' by Jacob Fichman, 'In the Jerusalem Hills' by Leah Goldberg, 'Jerusalem Nocturne' by Sister Marie-Madeleine (Hélène Jung), 'Isaac' by Nidaa Khouri, 'From Jerusalem: A First Poem' by Gabriel Preil, 'My City' by Miriam Tal, 'Jerusalem' by Nathan Yonatan.

To Shirley Kaufman for: 'To Jerusalem My City', 'He'll take you with Him', 'All Ordinary Things', all by Amir Gilboa (Menard Press); 'What's Not in the Heart' by Abba Kovner.

Linda Zisquit translated Sakinat al-Quds by Roger Tavor.

In London my gratitude to: Norman Morris who, not only in his capacity as Director of the Balfour Diamond Jubilee Trust, but also as a friend and counsellor, helped me throughout the making of this book; and to the Balfour Diamond Jubilee Trust, who gave me a financial grant towards travelling expenses.

Rabbi Hugo Gryn wrote the Introduction to 'If I Forget Thee' and contributed generously his time and knowledge. For his patience, kindness and humanity, my warmest thanks.

Bishop John Taylor, formerly Bishop of Winchester, and his wife Peggy gave me at all times their warm and kind encouragement and afforded several enjoyable visits to Oxford.

To a Jerusalem friend here in London.

I am indebted to Peter Levi who kindly gave me permission to use his translation of some of the Psalms in this book.

At the Leo Baeck College, Dr. Hyam Maccoby and Professor Israel Ben Yosef gave me help with scholarly advice, and Roy Seigal assisted me in the library.

Sheila Rosenberg gave me helpful and constructive advice, and Dr. James Holland helped with translation.

Frederick Marns, defying the elements, refined the design of the book and offered his expert and dependable help. I must also thank Joshua Kuperard for his help and friendliness; Dorothy Boux, Lady

Mavis Coulson and Valerie Petts for tea and sympathy and much else. Melisa Treasure gave me invaluable assistance. For her constant encouragement, for her creative criticism, for her sense of humour, badly needed by me at times, and for her friendship — my friendship always.

With special warmth to Beryl Bjelke, for her precious gift of friendship.

To my publisher Anthony Werner.

And, finally, for putting up with my elation — and occasional disheartenment — for three long years ... for their constant and loving support, my husband Paul, my children Clive, Danielle and Marc, and my family in Switzerland.

For permission to include material of which they control the copyright, grateful acknowledgement is made to the following:

Princeton University Press for excerpts from 'The Prism of Sennacherib' and 'The Story of Sinuhe the Egyptian' from *The Ancient Near East* edited by James B. Pritchard

Penguin Books Ltd for extracts from *The Psalms* translated by Peter Levi © 1976, Penguin Classics 1976

Atrium Press Ltd for *The Legend of the Third Dove* by Stefan Zweig

International Thomson Publishing Services Ltd for an extract from *The Way of Man (According to the Teaching of Hasidism)* by Martin Buber

David Higham Associates Ltd for 'The Sources of my Being' by Moses Ibn Ezra, and extracts from 'Longing for Zion', 'Lord, where shall I find you', and 'The Poet is urged to stay in Spain' by Judah ha-Levi from *The Jewish Poets of Spain* (Penguin Books), translated by David Goldstein

Harper and Row Publishers Inc and Olwyn Hughes for two poems by Yehuda Amichai, 'If I forget Thee, Jerusalem' and 'The Windmill in Yemin Moshe', the former from *Poems* translated by Assia Gutman, © 968, 1969 by Assia Gutman, the latter from *The Great Tranquility* translated by Glenda Abramson and Tudor Parfitt, © 1983 by Yehuda Amichai

Jewish Publication Society for 'Shulamite', 'Reconciliation' and 'My People' from *Hebrew Ballads and other Poems* by Else Lasker-Schuler

Twayne Publishers for a portion of the Introduction from *The Flowering of Modern Hebrew Literature* (1959) by Menachem Ribalow (trans. Judah Nadich)

Cambridge University Press, the Crown's patentee, for extracts from the Authorised Version of the *Bible* (The King James Bible), the rights of which are vested in the Crown

Oxford and Cambridge University Presses for an extract from *The New English Bible* © 1970

SCM Press Ltd for an extract from *Wisdom in Israel* by Gerhard von Rad translated by James D. Martin, 1972

Elie Wiesel for a short extract from *Legends of our Time*

Soncino Press Ltd for an extract from *The Zohar* translated by Harry Sperling and Maurice Simon, © 1984

ACUM Ltd for 'To the Sun' by Saul Tchernikowsky and 'Wedge Me into the Fissure' by Yehuda Karni, translated by Institute for the Translation of Hebrew Literature, Israel

University of California Press for 'Canopy in the Desert' and 'What's not in the Heart' by Abba Kovner, 'Jerusalem' by David Rokeah, 'Guard me, Oh God' and 'Ishmael, my Brother' by Shin Shalom, 'Tiller of the Soil' and 'Shepherd' by Abraham Shlonsky from *Modern Hebrew Poetry: A Bilingual Anthology* edited and translated by Ruth Finer Mintz

Dvir Publishing, Tel-Aviv for Chaim Nachman Bialik's poem 'The Scroll of Fire' from *Selected Poems: Bilingual Edition*, 1981, translation by Ruth Nevo

Penguin Books USA Inc. for 'They' by Mani Leyb from *The Penguin Book of Modern Yiddish Verse* by Irving Howe, Ruth Wisse and Chone Shmeruk, © 1987 by Irving Howe, Ruth Wisse and Chone Shmeruk. Translation by John Hollander, © 1987 by Irving Howe, Ruth Wisse and Chone Shmeruk. All rights reserved.

The publishers have made every effort to trace all copyright owners. If any have been overlooked, we offer our apologies and undertake to make proper acknowledgement in any reprint.

IN the Book of Genesis there is written the story of the first dove and also of the second, which the patriarch Noah sent forth out of the Ark, when the windows of heaven were stopped and the waters of the deep abated. Yet who has told of the travels and the destiny of the third dove? The ship of salvation, carrying within it all life that was spared from the flood, had grounded upon the peak of Mount Ararat, but the patriarch from his mast-head could see nought save the rise and fall of an infinity of water; he therefore sent out a dove, the first dove, to bring him news of any land that might be seen beneath the lowering skies.

The first dove, so we are told, soared upwards and spread her wings. She flew to the East and to the West, but the waters were everywhere. She found no rest for the sole of her foot and gradually her wings began to weaken. So she returned to the one firm place on earth, to the Ark, and she fluttered about the ship which rested on the mountain peak, until Noah put forth his hand, and took her, and pulled her in unto him into the Ark.

Now he waited for seven days, seven days in which no rain fell and the waters sank; then he took another dove, the second, and sent her out to search. The dove flew out in the morning and when she returned at the eventide she bore in her bill an olive leaf, the first sign that the earth was uncovered once again. Thus Noah learned that the treetops were already clear of the water and that the trial was surmounted.

After another seven days he once again sent forth a dove, the third, and she flew out into the world. In the morning she set forth, yet by evening she had not returned, and though Noah awaited her day after day, she never came back. Thus our ancestor knew that the earth was free and the waters sunken away. But of that dove, the third dove, he never heard again, nor did mankind either, for her legend has not been revealed until to-day.

These were the travels and the destiny of the third dove. In the morning she had flown forth from the ship's musty hold, where the beasts, crowded in darkness, stirred impatiently, hoof to claw, amidst a confusion of roaring and whistling, hissing and lowing; from confinement she flew forth into the infinity of space, from darkness into light. And when she spread her wings in the clear, clean air washed sweet by the rain she felt at once the freedom that was all about her and the grace of boundlessness. The waters of the deep glistened, the forests shone green as dewy moss, the mists of dawn drifted white across the meadows and those meadows were sweetly scented by the opening blossoms. Brightness poured down from the metallic sky to be mirrored below, so that the rising sun was reflected in a pink, eternal dawn upon the rocky mountain tops, while the sea shone blood-red and the flowering earth, too, steamed warm as blood. It was god-like to watch this awakening, and in an ecstasy of vision the dove floated across the purple world; easily she flew over lands and seas and in her dream slowly became herself a gliding dream. Like God Himself she was now the first to see the earth set free and there was no end to her looking. She had long ago forgotten Noah, the white-bearded captain of the Ark, she had forgotten her mission, she had forgotten that she must return. For the world was now her home, the heavens her very own house.

And so the third dove, the patriarch's faithless messenger, flew across the empty world, on and ever onwards, borne up by the violence of her joy, by the wind of her blissful unrest, ever onwards until her pinions grew heavy and her feathers leaden. The earth drew her down towards itself with a mighty force, her tired wings sank lower and lower so that already they grazed the damp treetops, and at last on the evening of the second day she settled down in the midst of a wood which, like everything else at time's beginning, was without a name. She hid deep in a thicket and rested from her journey through the skies. The twigs sheltered her, the breeze lulled her, the wood was cool by day and a warm dwelling-place by night. She soon forgot the windy heavens and the call of far places; embowered in the green trees, time grew over her, unreckoned.

It was a wood of the world close to us that the last dove had chosen for her home, but there were as yet no human beings within it, and in this solitude she gradually became a dream unto herself. In the darkness, in the green shade she nestled and the years passed her by and death forgot her, for of all those beasts — two of each breed which had seen the first world before the flood — none can ever die nor be harmed by the hunter. Invisible, they shelter in the hidden folds of earth's garment, and even so did this dove live deep in the forest. Sometimes, it is true, forebodings of the presence of man would reach her; a shot would ring out and be re-echoed a hundredfold from the walls of green; axes would be driven into the trunks so that the encircling darkness groaned; the soft laughter of lovers as they stole away together was a murmur in the undergrowth, and the songs of children picking berries came thinly from afar. The lost dove, enmeshed in foliage and in dream, sometimes heard those wordly voices, but they caused her no fear and she remained in her darkness.

But one day the whole wood began to roar and crack as though the very world were falling apart. Black masses of metal screamed through the air and where they fell the earth leapt up in horror and the trees were snapped like grasses. Men in coloured clothes hurled death at one another and fearful machines sprewed forth fire and flame. Lightning shot up from earth to clouds and after it thunder; it was as though the land wished to jump into the sky, or the sky to fall upon the land. The dove awakened from her dream. Death was all about her, and destruction; as once the water, so now fire was spread across the world. Quickly she stretched her wings and fluttered upwards, in search of a new home to replace her crashing, crackling wood, in search of a place where there was peace.

She fluttered upwards and flew across our world in search of peace, but go where she would she found everywhere the same man-made lightning, the same man-made thunder, everywhere was war. A sea of fire and blood had once again engulfed the earth, another flood had come, and quickly she flew across the land, searching for a place of rest whence she might return to the patriarch bearing the olive leaf of promise in her bill. But in these days none was to be found, ever higher rose the tide of ruin over mankind, while the flames raced ever on across the face of our world. She has not yet found a restingplace, nor humanity peace, and until then she may not return home, she may not be for ever still.

No man has seen her, the lost and mystical dove in her search for peace, but still she flutters over our heads, frightened and with pinions that are already weary. Sometimes, deep in the night, a man awakening from a startled sleep may hear wings beating high in the air, haste in darkness, anguished, unheeding flight. Upon her is the weight of all our sombre thoughts, in her fear are carried all our wishes, and there, fluttering between heaven and earth, is the lost dove. It is our own destiny that she now must learn, that she now must bear back, that faithless messenger of long ago, to the patriarch of mankind. And once again, as those thousands of years ago, the world is waiting, waiting that a hand be put forth to take her, waiting for the knowledge that the trial has been at last enough.

Stefan Zweig

In the Beginning

God, God the Lord hath spoken and called the earth
from the rising of the sun unto the going down thereof.
Out of Zion, the perfection of beauty, God hath shined forth.

(Psalm 50)

Thou art wise. And wisdom is the fount of life and
    from Thee it welleth,
And by the side of Thy wisdom all human knowledge
    turneth to folly.
Thou art wise, more ancient than all primal things,
And wisdom was the nursling at Thy side.
Thou art wise, and Thou hast not learnt from any
    beside Thee,
Nor acquired wisdom from any save Thyself.

Thou art wise, and from Thy wisdom Thou hast set
    apart Thy appointed purpose,
Like a craftsman and an artist
To draw up the films of Being from Nothingness
As light is drawn that darteth from the eye:
Without bucket from the fountain of light hath Thy
    workman drawn it up,
And without tool hath he wrought,
Hewing, graving, cleansing, refining,
Calling unto the void and it was cleft,
And unto existence and it was urged,
And to the universe and it was spread out;
Establishing the clouds of the heavens
And with his hand joining together the pavilions of
    the spheres,
And fastening with the loops of power the tent-folds
    of creation,
For the might of his hand extendeth to the uttermost
    borders,
"Linking the uttermost ends."

Solomon Ibn Gabirol

This expanse that spreads its nostrils wide.
This height that yearns to you overhead.
Light spilling the milk's white.
Fragrance of wool. Fragrance of bread.

At the feet of the sheep and man that listens,
In the water trough is the lapping tune —
Barefoot,
With all his five senses bared,
Morning steps toward noon.

This morn of Creation! Wafts in the fields
Incense from dung, dew drops from grass.
From horizon to horizon: Adam and fields.
From horizon to horizon: Abel and flocks.

Camel and plow. The sharp blade
Wearies cleaving clod from clod.
Never before was the world so one.
All eternities in that moment joined.

This is hint of murder,
This is plunged blade,
This is Cain who splits the clod's unity.
Never before was the distance so small
Between man
And camel
And sky.

Abraham Shlonsky

Now the Lord had said unto Abram, Get thee out of thy country, and from thy kindred, and from thy father's house, unto a land that I will shew thee:

And I will make of thee a great nation, and I will bless thee, and make thy name great; and thou shalt be a blessing:

So Abram departed, as the Lord had spoken unto him ... and into the land of Canaan they came.

(Genesis 12)

It was a good land. Figs were in it, and grapes.
It had more wine than water. Plentiful was its
honey, abundant its olives. Every fruit was on
its trees. Barley was there, and emner. There was
no limit to any cattle.

(The story of Sinuhe the Egyptian)

And Melchizedek king of Salem brought forth bread and wine: and he was the priest of the most high God.

And he blessed him, and said, Blessed be Abram of the most high God, Creator of heaven and earth.

(Genesis 14)

… and the Lord appeared into Abram and said, Thou shalt no more be called Abram, but thy name shall be Abraham; for a father of many nations have I made thee. And I will give unto thee, and thy seed after thee, the land of Canaan for an everlasting possession; and I will be their God.

(Genesis 17)

And Jacob was left alone; and there wrestled a man with him until the breaking of the day.
And when he saw that he prevailed not against him ... said, Let me go, for the day breaketh. And he said, I will not let thee go, except thou bless me.
And he said unto him, What is thy name? And he said, Jacob.
And he said, Thy name shall be called no more Jacob, but Israel

(Genesis 32)

Now an angel of the Lord appeared to
Moses in a blazing fire -

a fire that devours fire;
a fire that burns in things dry and moist;
a fire that glows amid snow and ice;
a fire that is like a crouching lion;
a fire that reveals itself in many forms;
a fire that is, and never expires;
a fire that shines and roars;
a fire that blazes and sparkles;
a fire that flies in a storm wind;
a fire that burns without wood;
a fire that renews itself every day;
a fire that is not fanned by fire;
a fire that billows like palm branches;
a fire whose sparks are flashes of lightning;
a fire black as a raven;
a fire, curled, like the colours of the rainbow!

Yannai

On this day Israel came to Mount Sinai

... he gave them knowledge
and bestowed on them the law of life.
He established an everlasting covenant with them
and told them of his laws.

(the Wisdom of Joshua Ben Sira)

When God gave the Law, no bird sang or flew, no ox bellowed,
the angels did not fly,
the Seraphim ceased from saying, 'Holy, holy',
the sea was calm, no creature spoke; the world was silent and
still, and the divine voice said:
'I am the Lord thy God; thou shalt have no other gods besides me.'

... the divine word descended from heaven, being on its way
engraved upon the four winds of the universe; and then
rose once more and again descended. When it rose up it
drew from the mountains pure balsam and was watered with
the heavenly dew, and when it reached this earth ... impressed
itself upon the tablets of stone, until the whole Ten Words
were designed thereon ... for each word was indeed like a
treasure-house, full of all precious things. And though when
one Word was uttered it sounded but as itself, yet when it
was stamped upon the stone seventy different aspects were
revealed in it ... and the souls of all the children of Israel,
past and present and to be, born and unborn, were present there,
that all might accept the Torah given on Mount Sinai.

(The Zohar)

So Moses went down unto the people,
and spake unto them

Longing I sought Thy presence;
Lord, with my whole heart did I call and pray,
And going out towards Thee,
I found Thee coming to me on the way.

Judah ha-Levi

Maike

Within thy Gates, O Jerusalem

Set me as a seal upon your heart ...
for love is as fierce as death,
passion is as harsh as the grave;
its flashes are raging fires, violent flames.
Vast floods cannot quench love,
nor can rivers sweep it away.

(*Song of Songs*)

You have spoken through a vision to your prophets,
you said, I have put power on a hero,
I have lifted up a man chosen from the people;
I have found David my servant,
I have anointed him with the oil of my holiness;
my hand will be fixed on him
and my arm will make him strong ...

He shall cry out to me, You are my father,
and my God, and the crag of my freedom.

(Psalm 89)

And the King and his men went to Jerusalem unto the Jebusites ... and
David took the strong hold of Zion and called it the city of David

Wake, lyre and harp;
I will wake at dawn and give thanks to you, O God,
    among the peoples,
I will sing the harp among the nations.
Because your love is above the heavens and your truth
    is like the sky.
O God, be high above the heavens, and your glory over
    the whole earth.

(Psalm 108)

I was glad because they said to me,
We shall go to the house of God.
We have set our feet in your gates, Jerusalem:
Jerusalem which is built as a city
united together in itself,
where the tribes come up, the tribes of God,
the witness of God to Israel to thank the name of God.
Because seats of judgement are in it,
the seats of the house of David.
Pray for the peace of Jerusalem;
those that love you shall prosper,
there shall be peace within your walls and prosperity in your houses.
Because of my brothers and my friends
I wish you peace.
Because of the house of God who is our God
I will pray for the good of Jerusalem.

(Psalm 122)

And it came to pass in the four hundred and eightieth year after the children of Israel were come out of the land of Egypt, in the fourth year of Solomon's reign over Israel . . . that he began to build the house of the Lord.

(1 Kings 6)

Now, the Temple, when it was finished, shone in the hour of evening like a golden hill set upon a silver mountain.

In the court, the altar of bronze increased that it might embrace the earth, the bath grew deeper that it might hold the waters of the sea. On the threshold the warp and woof of the curtains caught the hyacinthine shadows of the air. Under the ceiling, the candlestick lighted the purples of flame. And the Cherubim waited with coupled wings until the Holy Ark, which was to be conducted hither into the Holy of Holies, in the next dawn, should sanctify the Sanctuary, and, like a new world, bind the old world to God.

And multitudes thronged upon the slopes of Mount Moriah. Some had come out of Golan forsaking her fertile waters, some had come down from Gilead, leaving their flocks, some had quitted lake Chinnereth and the fish. Some abandoned the River Jordan, where the water tumbles and rushes, or the Dead Sea, where the waters lie salt and still. Others left blue Galilee, evergreen Carmel, Gilgal's blanched oasis, or Sharon's rosy plains. They came from Jericho, where the palm trees bear honey-sweet fruit; they came from Sodom, where the apple trees drop fruit bitter as ashes; from Hebron, honeycombed with caves and from Beersheba that burrows into the wilderness.

And they came, leading sheep and ewes, she-goats and young kids, bullocks and kine. And they came bearing corn and barley, pomegranates and grapes, figs and olives. They brought, every man according to his substance. And that they might offer their offerings in the Temple, they awaited the hour of dawn, when Solomon, escorting the Ark, should himself make offering of the Temple to the Eternal. And they were joyful and mingling their joy with the blessed night, they sang the songs of David.

Edmond Fleg

And God gave Solomon wisdom and understanding exceeding much, and largeness of heart, even as the sand that is on the sea shore.

And Solomon's wisdom excelled the wisdom of all men.

And he spake three thousand proverbs; and his songs were a thousand and five.

And he spake of trees, from the cedar tree that is in Lebanon even unto the hyssop that springeth out of the wall; he spake also of beasts, and of fowl, and of creeping things, and of fishes.

And there came of all people, to hear the wisdom of Solomon, from all kings of the earth, which had heard of his wisdom.

And he had peace on all sides round about him.

And Judah and Israel dwelt safely, every man under his vine and under his fig tree, from Dan to Beersheba, all the days of Solomon.

And the time that Solomon reigned in Jerusalem over all Israel was forty years.

And Solomon slept with his fathers, and was buried in the city of David his father.

(1 Kings 4-11)

*Now in the fourteenth year of King Hezekiah did Sennacherib King of Assyria
come up against all the fenced cities of Judea, and took them.*

As to Hezekiah, the Jew, he did not submit to my yoke, I laid siege to 46 of his
strong cities ... Himself I made a prisoner in Jerusalem, his royal residence,
like a bird in a cage.
I surrounded him with earthwork in order to molest those who were leaving his
city's gate.

(the Prism of Sennacherib)

And when Hezekiah saw that Sennacherib was come, and that he was
purposed to fight against Jerusalem, he took counsel with his princes and his
mighty men ... saying, Why should the kings of Assyria come, and find much
water? And he stopped the upper watercourse of Gihon, and brought it
straight down to the west side of the city of David.

(2 Chron. 32)

'This is the story of the boring through: whilst (the tunnelers lifted) the pick
each towards his fellow and whilst three cubits (yet remained) to be bored
(through, there was heard) the voice of a man calling his fellow, for there was a
split in the rock on the right hand and on (the left hand). And on the day of the
boring through, the tunnellers struck, each in the direction of his fellows, pick
against pick. And the water started to flow from the source to the pool, twelve
hundred cubits. A hundred cubits was the height of the rock above the head of
the tunnellers.'

*Nebuchadnezzar King of Babylon
came with all his army against
Jerusalem and laid siege to it …*

All night seas of flame raged and tongues of fire darted above the Temple Mount. Stars splintered from the baked skies and melted into the earth, spark after spark. Has God kicked his throne aside, and smashed his crown to smithereens?

Torn clouds reddened, laden with blood and fire. They went astray in the wide night and poured out the rage of a jealous God among the distant mountains, the tale of his fury among the desert rocks. Has God torn his purple mantle and scattered the rags to the wind?

The fear of God was upon the distant mountains, terror seized the sullen rocks of the desert. A revengeful God was the God that was revealed.

Here is the God of revenges, He himself. Calm and terrible he sits upon a throne of fire in an ocean of flame. His cloak is a purple pyre and his footstool burning coals. Small racing flames crown him, a cruel dance blazes around him. Above his head flame thirstily gulps the space of the world. Calm and terrible he sits with his arms crossed over his heart. Conflagration spreads at a glance of his eye, bonfires leap at a flicker of his eyelashes. Bring the Lord galloping chargers, bring the Lord a fierce fire dance.

And when dawn broke upon the hills and a pale vapour covered the valleys, the flames slackened and the tongues of fire sank back from the burnt sanctuary on the Temple Mount.

And when the angels gathered in holy concourse as they always did, to sing a song of dawn, they threw wide the windows of heaven and looked towards the Temple Mount to see whether the doors of the sanctuary were open, and whether the smoke of incense spiralled from them.

And they saw the Lord of Hosts, the ancient of days, sitting in the twilight of dawn upon desolation. His cloak was a cloud of smoke and his footstool dust and ashes. His head was bowed between his arms, and mountains of sorrow were heaped on his head. In silent desolation he sat and stared at the ruins. A cosmic rage lowered from his brows, there was a great frozen stillness in his eyes.

The Temple Mount still smoked. Piles of ash, mounds of cinders, smouldering brands lay all in heaps; hissing embers tumbled together glowed like stacks of carbuncle and jacinth in the silence of dawn.

And the fire-lion that crouches on the altar day and night — he took, was quenched. A single orphaned curl from the end of his mane gleamed fitfully and died on the pile of scorched stones in the silence of dawn.

The angels knew what God had done to them and they were shocked. They trembled, together with all the morning stars; and they covered their faces with their wings for they feared to look on the sorrow of God.

Their song that morning was a hushed lament, the murmur of a still small voice. Silently they turned away and wept, each angel alone, and all the world wept with them in the silence.

And a long deep sigh rose from the corners of the earth, rose and spread out, and broke upon the silent weeping. It was the world's heart breaking, and God could bear it no longer. He got up and roared like a lion, and clapped his hands, and the Shekinah rose from the ruins and went and hid herself.

The morning star shone furtively, mournfully, upon the Temple Mount. She gazed out from brilliant blue upon the ruins, and her lashes, silver lashes, quivered in the silence. One young angel, sad-eyed and clean-winged, guardian of the pearls that are in hidden tears, which he collects in the cup of speechless sorrow, saw the curl of fire above the morning star, the remnant of the lion of God, as it gleamed, quivered and died on the scorched stones of the Temple Mount.

And the angel was exceedingly troubled lest this last ember of God go out, and the holy fire vanish from the earth and be lost to the people of God and to his house for ever.

In great haste he flew over the morning star, a kerchief of fire in his hand, and landed on the rubble of the Temple Mount. Anxiously he made his way to the altar and raked the ashes for the fire of God. Then he spread his wings and flew away.

The pearl of a tear fell from the angel's eye and sank hissing into the pile of embers. It was the only pearl the angel had ever taken from the cup of speechless sorrow — a tear of relief and compassion at the saving of the remnant of the fire of God.

The angel glided between the mist of purity and the fire of holiness in his right hand. He clutched it to his heart and put it to his lips. In front of him the morning star danced, and his heart was full of hope and solace.

And he brought it to a desert island and placed it there on the summit of a massive rock. He raised his sad eyes and his lips whispered in the silence: 'God of mercies and deliverance! Do not extinguish your last light for ever.'

And God understood the clean-winged angel and rekindled the fire and commanded the morning star: 'Take care, my daughter, of my fire. Do not let it go out for it is the apple of my eye. Stay and see what will become of it.'

The morning star stood still in the heavens opposite the little flame, and beckoned to it from far off in dumb love and secret yearning. And she guarded it on the desert island, greeting it every morning with her radiance and visiting upon it her beams of mercy and comfort.

And the young sad-eyed angel flew back to his place to look after the hidden tears in the cup of speechless sorrow as before. But his eyes had grown deeper and sadder, and his heart and his lips were scorched — a wound which would never heal, for he had been touched beyond cure by the touch of the holy fire.

Hayyim Nahman Bialik

By the rivers of Babylon, there we sat down, yea, we wept, when we
    remembered Zion.
We hanged our harps upon the willows in the midst thereof.
For there they that carried us away captive required of us a song; and
they that wasted us required of us mirth, saying, Sing us one of the songs
    of Zion.
How shall we sing the Lord's song in a strange land?
If I forget thee, O Jerusalem, let my right hand forget her cunning.
If I do not remember thee, let my tongue cleave to the roof of my mouth;
    if I prefer not Jerusalem above my chief joy.

(Psalm 137)

49

In the twenty-fifth year of our exile ... the hand of the Lord came upon me and he brought me there. He brought me, in visions of God, to the Land of Israel, and He set me on a very high mountain on which there seemed to be the outline of a city on the south. He brought me over to it, and there, standing at the gate, was a man who shone like copper. In his hand were a cord of linen and a measuring rod. The man spoke to me: 'Mortal, look closely and listen attentively and note well everything I am going to show you — for you have been brought here in order to be shown — and report everything you see to the House of Israel.'

Then he led me to a gate, a gate that faced east. And there, coming from the east with a roar like the roar of mighty waters, was the Presence of the God of Israel, and the earth was lit up by His Presence.

The Presence of the Lord entered the Temple by the gate that faced eastward.

A spirit carried me into the inner court, and lo, the Presence of the Lord filled the Temple; and I heard speech addressed to me from the Temple, though the man was standing beside me. It said to me:

'O mortal, this is the place of My throne and the place for the soles of My feet, where I will dwell in the midst of the people of Israel forever ... You, O mortal, describe the Temple to the House of Israel, and let them measure its design. Such are the instructions for the Temple on the top of the mountain: the entire area of its enclosure shall be most holy ...'

(Ezekiel 40)

In the first year of King Cyrus of Persia ... the Lord roused the spirit of King Cyrus to issue a proclamation throughout his realm by word of mouth and in writing as follows:

'Thus said King Cyrus of Persia: The Lord of Heaven has given me all the kingdoms of the earth and has charged me with building Him a house in Jerusalem, which is in Judah. Anyone of you of all His people — may his God be with him, and let him go up to Jerusalem that is in Judah and build the House of the Lord the God of Israel, the God that is in Jerusalem.'

(Ezra 1)

And I arose in the night, I and some few men with me; neither told I
any man what my God put into my heart to do for Jerusalem;
neither was there any beast with me, save the beast that I rode upon.
And I went out by night by the valley gate, even toward the jackal's
well, and to the dung gate, and viewed the walls of Jerusalem, which
were broken down and the gates thereof were consumed with fire.
Then I went on to the fountain gate and to the king's pool; but there
was no place for the beast that was under me to pass. Then I went
up in the night by the brook, and viewed the wall; and I turned back,
and entered by the valley gate, and so returned. And the rulers knew
not whither I went, or what I did; neither had I as yet told it to the
Jews, nor the priests, nor the nobles, nor to the rulers, nor to the rest
that did the work ...
Then said unto them, come, and let us build up the wall of Jerusalem,
that we be no more a reproach ... And they said, Let us rise up and build.

(Nehemia 2)

In the reign of Artaxerxes king of Persia, Ezra ... went up from Babylon.
Ezra had prepared his heart to seek the law of the Lord, and to do it, and
to teach in Israel statutes and judgments.

(Ezra 7)

My people, listen to my law,
hear what I say.
I will tell a story,
I will speak in old sayings.
We know them, they are familiar,
we have heard them from our fathers.
We shall not keep them secret from our children,
we shall tell the new generation the praises of God,
his power, and the wonders of his work.

(Psalm 78)

I wakened my thoughts from slumber
To put to sleep the desire of my heart and eyes.
And the vagaries of Fortune I perused in my mind
To attune my ears to the events to come.
And the mouth of my thought told me great things,
And placed before me the wondrous deeds of my Lord,
And told me the inaccessible mysteries,
Until I thought I was neighbour to the sons on high.
A vision of the Almighty took hold of my mind,
And I knew that within me there was God.
His magnificent splendour was hidden,
But he was revealed in deed before the eyes of thought.
In my body he has kindled a lamp from his glory;
It tells me of the paths of the wise.
It is the light which shines in the days
Of youth, and grows brighter in old age.
Were it not derived from the mystery of his light
It would fail with my strength and my years.
With it I search out the chamber of wisdom,
And I climb with no ladder to the garden of delights...

The wisdom of the departed I regard as my portion,
And their writings are a balm to my sorrow,
And among them I hold sweet discourse,
Since they are the choicest of the faithful.
And when I swim in the sea of their wisdom
I gather pearls to embroider the days,
And in them is the delight of my eyes and heart,
And of them my jubilating lips will sing —
The light of my eyes, the song in my ears, the honey in
    my mouth,
And in my nostrils the scent of cinnamon.
And of them I shall muse, and be exalted all my days,
For in them are the sources of my being.

Moses Ibn Ezra

Hellenism and Roman Power

I was to my god like a hyacinth, or a violet,
    Like a bright sheaf of gold in the heavy wild corn;
    And he brought me warm mists on a cold mountain morn,
Symphonies of light and shade, blue, calm and scarlet.

I grasped the time's sorrow, heard the songs men create —
    Voices shedding light, in alien darkness crying:
    Between the living and those already dying,
Had I come too early or was my creator late?

Still in my heart sleeps dew that falls on Edom's sod,
High on the holy mount, home of the primal god,
    For my heart murmurs songs to sun and Orion.

When pods burst, fruit ripen, and leaves of saplings sprout,
A dead world's idols grab me, and there's no way out —
    Or a last statue from the age of the lion?

Saul Tchernichowsky

The story of the Septuagint

Demetrius of Phalerum, as keeper of the king's library, received large grants of public money with a view to his collecting, if possible, all the books in the world; and by purchases and transcriptions he to the best of his ability carried the king's purpose into execution. Being asked once in my presence, about how many thousands of books were already collected, he replied 'More than two hundred thousand, O king; and I will ere long make diligent search for the remainder, so that a total of half a million may be reached.

'*To the great king from Demetrius* — In obedience to thy order, O king, that the books which are wanting to complete the library should be added to the collection, and that those which are defective should be duly repaired, I have expanded great care upon these matters and now submit a reference to thee. The books of the Jewish law with some few others are wanting. They are written in Hebrew letters and in the Hebrew tongue, and have been interpreted somewhat carelessly and do not represent the original text, according to information supplied by the experts, because they have never received a king's fostering care. It is necessary that these books too should in an emended form find a place in thy library, because this code of laws, in that it is divine, is full of wisdom and faultless. For this reason authors, poets and the mass of the historians have abstained from any mention of the books aforesaid and of the men who have lived [and are living] in accordance with them, because the views presented in them have a certain sanctity and holiness, as says Hecataeus of Abdera. If then it be *thy* good pleasure, O king, a letter shall be written to the high priest at Jerusalem, bidding him send six elders from each tribe, men of the highest repute and versed in their country's law, in order that we may test wherein the more part agree, and so obtaining an accurate translation may deposit it in a conspicuous place in a manner worthy of the undertaking and of thy gracious will. Fare ever well!'

'*King Ptolemaeus to Eleazar the high priest greeting and health.*

'Forasmuch as there are many Jews settled in our realm who were forcibly removed from Jerusalem by the Persians at the time of their power, and others who entered Egypt as captives in the train of our father — of these he enrolled many of the army, giving them higher than the ordinary pay, and in like manner, having proved the loyalty of those who were already in the country, he placed under their charge the fortresses which he built ... and we too since ascending the throne meet all men, but chiefly thy countrymen, in a very friendly spirit — we, then, have given liberty to more than a hundred thousand captives ...

Our intent in this was to do a pious action and to dedicate a thank-offering to the Most High God, who has preserved our kingdom in peace and in the highest esteem throughout the whole world. Moreover, we have drafted into the army those who are in the prime of life, and to such as are fitted to be attached to our person and deserving of the confidence of court have we assigned offices of state. Now since we desire to confer a favour not on these only, but on all Jews throughout the world and on future generations, it is our will that your Law be translated from the Hebrew tongue in use among you into Greek, that so these writings also may find a place in our library with the other royal volumes. Thou wilt therefore do well and wilt repay our zeal, if thou lookest out six elders from each tribe, men of high repute, well versed in the Law and able to translate, that we may discover wherein the more part agree; for the investigation concerns matters of more than ordinary import. We think to gain great renown by the fulfilment of this task. We have sent on this business Andreas, of the chief of the bodyguards, and Aristeas, who hold honoured places in our court, to confer with thee. They bring with them dedicatory offerings for the temple, and for sacrifices and other purposes an hundred talents of silver. And shouldest thou also write to us concerning my desires, thou wilt do a favour and a friendly service; and be assured that thy wishes will receive instant fulfilment. Farewell.'

(The Letter of Aristeas)

On their arrival they were invited to a banquet and entertained and feasted their host in return with clever and earnest speeches. For he made trial of each man's wisdom, propounding novel and unusual questions, while they, the occasion not permitting of a long discourse, solved the conundrums which were put to them with the ready sagacity and pointed repartee of the speaker of terse apophthegms.

After passing this scrutiny, they proceeded straightway to discharge the duties of their honourable embassy; and reflecting with one another upon the magnitude of the task of giving an oracular interpretation of divinely inspired laws, being under constraint neither to detract ought nor to add nor to transpose, but to preserve their original form and type, they looked for the purest spot in the district, without the city ... The island of Pharos lies in front of Alexandria; its neck of land with half-submerged sandbanks stretches along over against the city and is washed by a sea which is not deep close inshore but for the most part consists of lagoons, so that the mighty roar and crash of the waves breaking a very great distance away are deadened. This spot out of all the surrounding district they selected as the most suitable haven wherein to find peace and quietness and for solitary communion between their souls and the laws. So here they abode, and taking the holy books they extended their hands with them to heaven, entreating God that they might not fail in their purpose. And He granted their prayers, in order that the more part, or indeed the whole, of the human race might reap the benefit of access, for the amendment of life, to *our* wise and wholly excellent ordinances.

In secret they sat, with none present save the elements of nature — earth, water, air, heaven — whose origin it was their first task to expound (for the cosmogony holds the first place in our laws); and, as men possessed, they produced not divers interpretations, but all alike used the same words and phrases, as though some invisible prompter whispered in the ears of each.

Philo Judaeus

Antiochus Epiphanes, son of King Antiochus, in the year [*169BC*] marched with a strong force against Israel and Jerusalem ... The king then issued a degree throughout his empire: his subjects were all to become one people and abandon their own laws and religion. The penalty for disobedience was death —

At this time a certain Mattathias, son of John, son of Symeon, appeared on the scene. He was a priest of the Joarib family from Jerusalem, who had settled at Modin. Mattathias had five sons ... they swept through the country.

Then Judas Maccabaeus came forward. He had the support of all his brothers and his father's followers, and they carried on the fight for Israel.

He spread his people's glory far and wide,
He donned a breastplate like a giant,
And girded on his weapons of war.
He organized battles, protecting his camp with the sword;
He was like a lion in his deeds,
Like a lion's whelp roaring for its prey ...
And deliverance was accomplished by his hand.

(l. Maccabees)

Judah assembled the people and said that after the many victories that God had given them, they ought to go up to Jerusalem and purify the Temple ...

He brought in new vessels, such as lampstand, table, and altar, and hung curtains from the doors, and replaced the doors themselves; he also pulled down the altar, and built a new one of various stones which had been hewn with iron. And on the twenty-fifth of the month Kislev, they kindled the lights on the lampstand and burned incense on the altar and set out the loaves on the table and offered offerings upon the new altar. These things, as it chanced, took place on the same day on which, three years before, their holy service had been transformed into an impure and profane form of worship. For the Temple, after being made desolate by Antiochus, had remained so for three years ...

And so Judah together with his fellow citizens celebrated for eight days, while honoring God with songs of praise and the playing of harps.

Josephus

When Vespasian came to destroy Jerusalem, he said to them, 'Fools, why do you seek to destroy this city, and to burn the Temple? All I want is that you deliver up to me one single bow and arrow, and then I will raise the siege.' They said, 'As we repelled the first and second attacks, and slew your men, so we will repel the next attack, and slay them.' When Rabbi Johanan heard this, he sent for the men of Jerusalem and said to them, 'Why would you lay waste this city and burn the Temple? All he seeks from you is one bow and arrow, and then he will retire.' They replied, 'As we repelled the first two attacks and killed his soldiers, so we will now go out against him and kill him.' Vespasian had men who watched beside the walls, and whatever they heard, they wrote upon arrows and threw them over the wall. So they told Vespasian that Rabbi Johanan was a friend of the Emperor. When Rabbi Johanan urged them for three days, and they refused, he called his disciples, and said, 'Up and carry me out of the city. Make a coffin and I will sleep in it.' They did so, and at the setting of the sun they brought it to the gates of Jerusalem. The gatekeeper said, 'What is this?' They said, 'A corpse is in it, and, as you know, a corpse must not be left in the city overnight,' so they said, 'If it be a corpse, carry it forth.' So they carried him forth, and brought him to Vespasian. Then they opened the coffin, and he stood before Vespasian. He said, 'Are you Rabbi Johanan b. Zakkai? What shall I give you?' He replied, 'All I ask of you is that I may go to Jabneh, and teach my disciples there, and fix a place of prayer there, and carry out all the commandments.' He answered, 'Go, and all that it pleases you to do there, do.'

(Aboth de Rabbi Nathan)

Christ, who in the reign of Tiberius,
was brought to punishment by Pontius
Pilate the procurator

Tacitus

And when the sabbath was past, Mary Magdalene, and Mary the mother of James, and Salome, had bought sweet spices, that they might come and anoint him. And very early in the morning the first day of the week, they came unto the sepulchre at the rising of the sun. And they said among themselves, Who shall roll us away the stone from the door of the sepulchre? And when they looked, they saw that the stone was rolled away: for it was very great. And entering into the sepulchre, they saw a young man sitting on the right side, clothed in a long white garment; and they were affrighted.

And he said unto them, Be not affrighted: Ye seek Jesus of Nazareth, which was crucified: he is risen; he is not here: behold the place where they laid him. But go your way, tell his disciples and Peter that he goeth before you into Galilee: there shall ye see him, as he said unto you. And they went out quickly, and fled from the sepulchre; for they trembled and were amazed: neither said they any thing to any man; for they were afraid.

(Mark 16)

Titus came to a place called Scopus, from whence the city began already to be seen, and a plain view might be taken of the great temple . . .

But Titus, intending to pitch his camp nearer to the city than Scopus . . . gave orders for the whole army to level the distance, as far as the wall of the city. So they threw down all the hedges and walls which the inhabitants had made about their gardens and groves of trees, and cut down all the fruit trees that lay between them and the wall of the city, and filled up all the hollow places and the chasms, and demolished the rocky precipices with iron instruments; and thereby made all the place level from Scopus to Herod's monuments.

The City of Jerusalem was fortified with three walls, on such parts as were not encompassed with unpassable valleys, for in such places it hath but one wall. The city was built upon two hills, which are opposite to one another, and have a valley to divide them asunder . . .

Now of these three walls, the old one was hard to be taken, both by reason of the valleys, and of that hill on which it was built, and which was above them. But besides that great advantage as to the place where they were situated, it was also built very strong; because David and Solomon, and the following kings, were very zealous about this work.

Now the towers that were upon it . . . were so very tall, they appeared much taller by the place on which they stood; for that very old wall was built upon an high hill, and was itself a kind of elevation that was still thirty cubits taller . . .

The largeness also of the stones was wonderful; for they were not made of common small stones, nor of such larger ones only as men could carry, but they were of white marble, cut out of the rock; each stone was twenty cubits in length and ten in breadth, and five in depth. They were so exactly united to one another, that each tower looked like one entire rock of stone, so growing naturally, and afterward cut by the hands of the artificers into their present shape and corners; so little, or not at all, did their joints or connections appear. Now as these towers were them-selves on the north side of the wall, the king had a palace inwardly thereto adjoined, which exceeds all my ability to describe it; for it was so very curious as to want no cost nor skill in its construction, but was entirely walled about to the height of thirty cubits, and was adorned with towers at equal distances, and with large bed-chambers, that would contain beds for an hundred guests a-piece, in which the variety of the stones is not be expressed; for a large quantity of those that were rare of that kind was collected together. Their roofs were also wonderful, both for the length of the beams, and the splendour of their ornaments. The number of the rooms was also very great, and the variety of the figures that were about them was prodigious; their furniture was complete, and the greatest part of the vessels that were put in them was of silver and gold. There were besides many porticoes, one beyond another, round about, and in each of those porticoes curious pillars; yet were all the courts that were exposed to the air every where green. There were moreover several groves of trees, and long walks through them, with deep canals and cisterns, that in several parts were filled with brazen statues, through which the water ran out. There were withal many dove-courts of tame pigeons about the canals.

Now this temple, as I have already said, was built upon a strong hill. At first the plain on the top was hardly sufficient for the holy house and the altar; for the ground about it was very uneven, and like a precipice; but when king Solomon, who was the person that built the temple, and built a wall to it, on its east side, there was then added one cloister, founded on a bank cast up for it, and on the other parts the holy house stood naked. But in future ages the people added new banks, and the hill became a larger plain.

As to the holy house itself, which was placed in the midst [of the inmost court] that most sacred part of the temple, it was ascended to by twelve steps.

Its first gate was seventy cubits high, and twenty-five cubits broad: but this gate had no doors, for it represented the universal visibility of heaven, and that it cannot be excluded from any place.

But then this house had golden doors of fifty-five cubits altitude, and sixteen in breadth; but before these doors there was a veil of equal largeness with the doors. It was a Babylonian curtain, embroidered with blue, and fine linen, and scarlet, and purple, and of a contexture that was truly wonderful. Nor was this mixture of colours without its mystical interpretation, but was a kind of image of the universe; for by the scarlet there seemed to be enigmatically signified fire, by the fine flax the earth, by the blue the air, and by the purple the sea; two of them having their colours the foundation of this resemblance; but the fine flax and the purple have their own origin for that foundation, the earth producing the one, and the sea the other. This curtain had also embroidered upon it all that was mystical in the heavens.

But the inmost part of the temple of all was of twenty cubits. This was also separated from the outer part by a veil. In this there was nothing at all. It was inaccessible and inviolable, and not to be seen by any and was called the Holy of Holies.

Now as soon as the army had no more people to slay or to plunder, because there remained none to be the objects of their fury, (for they would not have spared any, had there remained any other such work to be done) Caesar gave orders that they should now demolish the entire city and temple, but should leave as many of the towers standing as were of the greatest eminency, that is Phasaelus, and Hippicus, and Mariamne, and so much of the wall as inclosed the city on the west side. This wall was spared, in order to afford a camp for such as were to lie in garrison, as were the towers also spared in order to demonstrate to posterity what kind of city it was, and how well fortified, which the Roman valour had subdued; but for all the rest of the wall, it was so thoroughly laid even with the ground by those that dug it up to the foundation, that there was left nothing to make those that came thither believe it had ever been inhabited.

Josephus Flavius

A cry is heard in Ramah —
Wailing, bitter weeping —
Rachel weeping for her children.
She refuses to be comforted
For her children, who are gone.

(Jeremiah 31)

He'll take you with him far away and there
under the willows you'll weep on knees
that don't support him any more. He can hardly breathe.
And from the weeping that keeps rising and falling
like verses from Lamentations
your pleasant son Ephraim will be born again to walk
in the mountains of his greenness. You will want
to imagine how he looks
but you'll have to be patient who knows
how many thousands of years before a dream will grow again
from the waste and desolation of the dwellings you left.
And everything you plowed will be covered by ruins
and the one who kept silent will raise you again
                                            from the plunder
to go toward the source of the sunrise
when it burns again, scarlet, as though you'd been seeing it
thousands of years. A thousand years more and its light
will strike your heart and its light will strike your face
till you weep to see your sins white as snow again
and you'll rise up and live

Amir Gilboa

Urbs Jerusalem Beata

"Next year in Jerusalem". It is by this affirmation, proclaimed each year at the end of the Passover Seder, that the hope of Israel has expressed itself for centuries. Certainty sharpened by nostalgia. Patience confirmed by duration. The People of the Promise have passed through exile, trusting, whatever the cost, in the Word summoning them.

We have seen the end of this long wait. "At last we have set our feet in your gates, Jerusalem". Henceforth, each son of Israel can make his the Psalmist's cry of joy.

And yet, contested by some, rejected by others, for many a sign of contradiction, has the return of the Jewish people to the Land of the Bible finally marked the end of exile? This question preys on Jewish consciousness and should prey on that of the world.

There is indeed a paradox that, sooner or later, those who live in Jerusalem come to experience: the city appears as a homeland and place of exile in one. She is the home to which one was aspiring but seems to offer only a halt in the desert. Home and motherland indeed: Jerusalem is the expression of dispersion and wandering. And yet, for those who have the daunting privilege of being her citizens, Jerusalem still is a land of exile.

This is first of all true both on a human and an earthly level. For many of those who go there with enthusiasm and fervor, the climate, the landscape, the surroundings, the language are not those of their native land. Deep in their hearts and minds still exists the nostalgia for a landscape, a patrimony, a culture, from which they feel exiled by a part of themselves.

And deeper still, whatever the light of Jerusalem, whatever the feeling of fulfilment brought by the grace of living there, the limits and contradictions of this city seems to engrave upon the hearts of those who live there the expectancy of another fulfilment. Homecoming has led to another exile.

We are so made that we perceive fulfilment and affirmation only through the experience of limit and contradiction. We discover the country of which we are citizens only through the feeling of exile. We anticipate the happiness to which we are called only through the nostalgia which is at the heart of our needs and our emptiness. "The rose alone is fragile enough to express eternity". Jerusalem is the privileged place of that experience.

Already it had been the experience of the Patriarchs of Israel, as described in the Epistle to the Hebrews: "These all died in faith, not having received the promises, but having seen them afar off, and were persuaded of them, and embraced them, and confessed that they were strangers and pilgrims on the earth. For they that say such things declare plainly that they seek a country. And truly, if they had been mindful of that country from whence they came out, they might have had opportunity to have returned. But now they desire a better country, that is an heavenly, wherefore God is not ashamed to be called their God, for He hath prepared for them a city".

A city whose earthly Jerusalem is at one and the same time the fulfilment and the annunciation.

In the same way that she is situated like a promontory, on the edge of the desert, on the line of division of the waters, Jerusalem stands at the border between the Orient and the Occident, between past and present. Furthermore this border line pierces her and threatens to tear her apart. In her, the sacred and the profane, holiness and sin, meet and confront each other. She belongs both to the everyday and to the transcendent, to the human and to the divine, to time and to eternity. City of stone and city of heaven, she is at the same time a city where men with their earthly passions live, and the symbol which foreshadows Jerusalem the Heavenly.

There is a word in the Christian vocabulary which describes adequately the meaning of Jerusalem: this city is a sacrament. Luminous or obscure, painful or uplifting, her earthly reality invites the discovery beyond herself of a transcendent reality. Jerusalem is the point in space and time where God has intervened in history for the salvation of man and where He continues to work.

Père Marcel Jacques Dubois

A hymn, O God becometh Thee in Sion
and a vow shall be paid to Thee in Jerusalem.

Te decet hymnus, Deus in Sion
et tibi reddetur votum in Jerusalem.

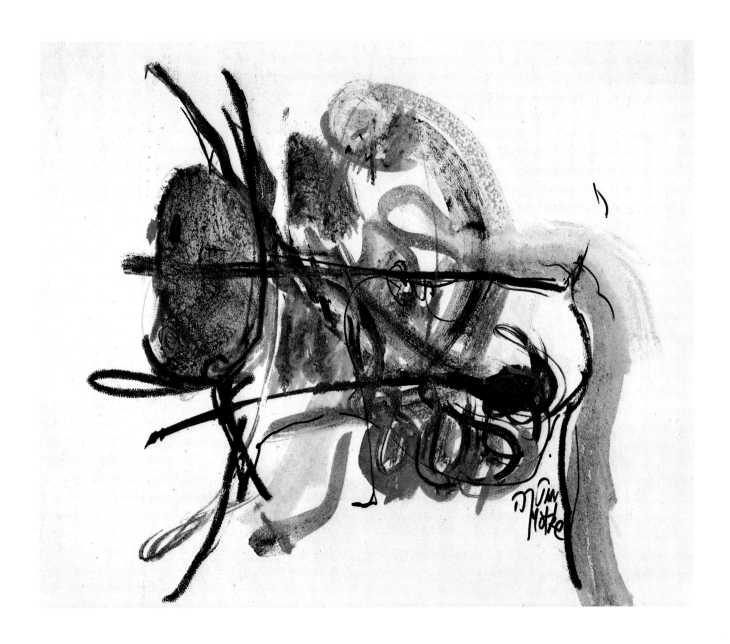

It was the practice of his parents to go to Jerusalem every year for the Passover festival; and when he was twelve, they made the pilgrimage as usual ...
after three days they found him in the Temple, sitting in the midst of the doctors, both hearing them, and asking them questions. And all that heard his were astonished as his understanding and answers

(Luke 2)

... and you, a wild olive, have been grafted in among them, and have come to share the same root and sap as the olive, do not make yourself superior to the branches.
If you do so, remember that it is not you who sustain the root: the root sustains you.

(Epistle to the Romans)

Thou shalt love the Lord thy God with all thy heart and with all thy soul

(Deuteronomy 6)

Thou shalt love thy neighbour as thyself

(Leviticus 19)

Hillel said:
What is hateful to you, do not to your fellow-creature

Be of the disciples of Aaron, loving peace and pursuing peace, loving thy fellow-creatures, and drawing them near to the Torah.

First thou shalt love the God who made thee,
secondly, thy neighbour as thyself;
and whatsoever thou wouldst not have done to
thyself, do not thou to another.

'There is none other commandment greater than
these,' Jesus had said of the first clause and
the second, and of the third, 'for this is the
Law and the Prophets.'

(the Didache)

I see thy Form, o lovely, mild Jerusalem Wing'd with Six Wings
In the opacous Bosom of the Sleeper, lovely, threefold
In Head and Heart and Reins, three Universes of love and beauty.
Thy forehead bright, Holiness to the Lord! with gates of pearl
Reflects Eternity beneath thy azure wings of feathery down,
Ribb'd, delicate, and cloth'd with feather'd gold and azure and
    purple,
From thy white shoulders shadowing purity in holiness;
Thence, feather'd with soft crimson of the ruby, bright as fire,
Spreading into the azure wings which, like a canopy,
Bends over thy immortal Head in which Eternity dwells.

Thy Bosom white, translucent, cover'd with immortal gems,
A sublime ornament not obscuring the outlines of beauty,
Terrible to behold, for thy extreme beauty and perfection:
Twelvefold here all the Tribes of Israel I behold
Upon the Holy Land: I see the River of Life and Tree of Life;
I see the New Jerusalem descending out of Heaven
Between thy Wings of gold and silver, feather'd immortal,
Clear as the rainbow, as the cloud of the Sun's tabernacle.

Thy Reins cover'd with Wings translucent, sometimes covering
And sometimes spread abroad, reveal the flames of holiness
Which like a robe covers, and like a Veil of Seraphim
In flaming fire unceasing burns from Eternity to Eternity.

William Blake

שלום
Motke

Hierusalem is seated on two hills
Of height unlike, and turned side to side,
The space between a gentle valley fills,
From mount to mount expansèd far and wide.
Three sides are sure imbarred with crags and hills,
The rest is easy, scant to rise espied:
    But mighty bulwarks fence that plainer part,
    So art helps nature, nature strengtheneth art.

The town is stored of troughs and cisterns, made
To keep fresh water, but the country seems
Devoid of grass, unfit for ploughman's trade,
Not fertile, moist with rivers, wells and streams;
There grow few trees to make the summer's shade,
To shield the parching land from scorching beams,
    Save that a wood stands six miles from the town,
    With aged cedars dark, and shadows brown.

By east, among the dusty valleys, glide
The silver streams of Jordan's crystal flood;
By west, the Midland Sea, with bounders tied
Of sandy shores, where Joppa whilom stood;
By north Samaria stands, and on that side
The golden calf was reared in Bethel wood;
    Bethlem by south, where Christ incarnate was,
    A pearl in steel, a diamond set in brass.

Torquato Tasso

Give me my scallop-shell of quiet,
my staff of Faith to walk upon,
My scrip of joy, immortal diet,
My bottle of salvation,
My gown of glory, hope's true gage,
And thus I'll take my pilgrimage.
                        Walter Ralegh

Loving sisters, since I know you are eager to know about the services they have daily in the holy places, I shall tell you about them ...

When it is the morning all the people assemble in their usual way in the Great Church, the Martyrium, and have sermons from the presbyters and then the bishop, and the offering is duly made in the way that is usual on the Lord's day, except that the dismissal at the Martyrium is hurried, so that it is over before nine o'clock. And soon after the dismissal at the Martyrium all the people escort the bishop with singing to Sion, where they arrive in time for nine o'clock ... the service proceeds as usual, and they make the offering there. Then as the people are dismissed the archdeacon makes this announcement: 'Let us all be ready today on the Mount of Eleona (that is, of Olives) at the Imbomon immediately after midday.'

So all the people return home for a rest. And as soon as they have had their meal, they go up to Eleona, the Mount of Olives, each at his own pace, till there is not a Christian left in the city. Once they have climbed Eleona, the Mount of Olives, they go first to the Imbomon, the place from which the Lord ascended into heaven, where the bishop and the presbyters take their seats, and likewise all the people. They have readings, and between them hymns and antiphons suitable to this day and to the place … When this has been done, the catechumens are blessed, and also the faithful.

It is now already three o'clock, and they go down singing hymns from there to another church, also on Olivet, and in it is the cave where the Lord used to sit and teach the Apostles. By the time they get there it is after four, and they have vespers. The prayer is said, the catechumens are blessed, and then the faithful.

Thence all the people go down with their bishop, singing hymns and antiphons suitable to the day, and so, very slowly and gently, they make their way to the Martyrium. When they arrive at the city gate it is already night, and the people are brought hundreds of church candles to help them. But since it is quite a way from the gate to the Great Church, the Martyrium, they arrive there at about eight at night, going very slowly all the way so that the walk does not weary the people. The great doors which face the market street are opened, and the bishop and all the people enter the Martyrium with hymns.

Once inside the church they have hymns and a prayer, and the catechumens are blessed, and also the faithful. Then they set off once more with hymns to the Anastasis. Again in the Anastasis they have more hymns and antiphons and a prayer, and the catechumens are blessed, and also the faithful. Then the same is done again at the Cross. And once more all the Christian community conducts the bishop with hymns to Sion. Once there, they have suitable readings, psalms, and antiphons, a prayer, the blessing of the catechumens and the faithful, and so they are dismissed. After the dismissal everyone goes to have the bishop's hand laid on him, and about midnight everybody returns to his home. Thus this is a very tiring day for them, for they have never stopped all day since they kept vigil in the Anastasis at cock-crow, and the services have taken so long that it is midnight by the time they are dismissed at Sion and all return to their homes.

(Egeria Pilgrimage)

The land which to that point had preserved some greenery grew naked, the slopes of the mountains grew steeper and took on an appearance that was at the same time more grand and more barren. Soon all vegetation ceased and even the moss disappeared. The mountains all round took on a red color. We climbed for an hour in this desolate landscape to reach a high pass that we spied before us. Once come to this pass, we journeyed for another hour across a naked plain strewn with boulders. Suddenly, at the end of this plain I saw a line of gothic walls flanked with square towers and behind them rose the peaks of buildings...

Then I understood what the historians and travellers reported of the surprise of the Crusaders and pilgrims at their first sight of Jerusalem. I am certain that whoever has had the patience, as I did, to read nearly two hundred modern accounts of the Holy Land, the rabbinic collections, and the passages of the ancients on Judea, would still understand nothing. I stood there, my eyes fixed on Jerusalem, measuring the height of its walls, recalling all the memories of history from Abraham to Godfrey of Bouillon, reflecting how the entire world was changed by the mission of the Son of Man, and seeking in vain the Temple, on which 'not a stone rests upon a stone'. If I were to live a thousand years, never would I forget this wilderness which still seems to breathe with the grandeur of Jehovah and the terrors of death.

The first travellers were fortunate; first, because they found in their readers a religious conviction which was never at odds with truth; secondly, because everyone was convinced that the only way to see a country as it truly is was to see it with all its traditions and memories. In effect it is with the Bible and the Gospels in hand that one should travel around the Holy Land. If one brings a contentious spirit to it, Judea is hardly worth the trouble of coming so far to visit ...

I had seen everything at Jerusalem; I knew the city inside and out so I began to take thought of my departure. The Fathers of the Holy Land ... begged me accept the Order of the Holy Sepulcher. This Order, which, without tracing it back to St. Helena, is a very old one in Christianity, was once widespread in Europe, but today is rarely encountered outside of Spain and Poland. The guardian of the Holy Sepulcher alone has the right to confer it.

At one o'clock we left the convent and went to the Church of the Holy Sepulcher. We went into the chapel that belongs to the Latin Fathers ... The guardian put on his pontifical vestments. The lamps were lit and all the Friars present formed a circle around me, their arms crossed upon their breasts. Whilst they chanted in a low voice the Veni Creator, the guardian went up to the altar and I knelt. They took out from the treasury of the Holy Sepulcher the spurs and the sword of Godfrey of Bouillon. Two religious knelt on either side of me holding these venerable relics. The officiating officer recited the customary prayers and then catechized me on certain customary practices. Then he fitted me with the spurs, struck me three times upon the shoulder with the sword while giving me the formal address. The religious chanted the Te Deum as the guardian said this prayer over me: 'Lord, God Almighty, shower Thy Grace and Blessings over this Thy servant, etc.' All of it was merely the remembrance of a way of life that no longer exists. But when you consider that I was in Jerusalem, in the church of Calvary, a dozen paces from the Tomb of Jesus Christ and no more than thirty from the tomb of Godfrey of Bouillon, that I had been vested with the spurs of the liberator of the Holy Sepulcher and touched with that long, wide sword of iron once wielded by a hand so noble and so loyal; when you recall the circumstances, my life filled with adventure, my travels on land and sea, you will understand that I could not but be moved ...

They gave me my patent, signed with the signature of the guardian and the seal of the convent. Together with this distinguished diploma of knighthood, I was given my humble certificate of pilgrimage. I am saving them as a memorial of my voyage into the land of the old traveller Jacob.

Chateaubriand

In the Church of the Holy Sepulchre
   on the balcony
the ringing of hammers to stone to metal to stone to wood
   the tuneless song   the din   my tears
the black-caped women and the black-robed men

In the Church of Wherever with the chess-board floor
   the hammering hymn and the whirlpool door
the question is unanswerable.
   We build a tower up from the flood
Pain is your companion. Am I then alone?

In the Church of Impossibility I come   to pray
and somewhere I am answered where I cannot see
and somehow I am answered what I cannot be
and terrible the strokes of the hammer:
   'Let me in'   'Let me in'

   A monk walks below   looks up: 'Mary!'
the lanterns   the hammers   the silent bells
   the arches   the light
   you ask for faith ...
I pray miracle love 'yes'
   and shudder   its cool
         The drinker paces in his trap
         The monk walks looking up
Who will sing OHM
and crash to the floor
   a broken bird
         blood
            staining eternity?

      Down from purgatory
                        or up?
                           I go up
Mater Dolorosa   holy child   giving birth
      praying at a grave ...

Hadassah Haskale

You never enjoy the World aright, till the sea itself floweth in your veins, till you are clothed with the heavens, and crowned with the stars: and perceive yourself to be the sole heir of the whole world, and more than so, because men are in it who are every one sole heirs as well as you ...

Till your spirit filleth the whole world, and the stars are your jewels, till you are familiar with the ways of God in all Ages as with your walk and table: till you are intimately acquainted with that shady nothing out of which the world was made: till you love men so as to desire their happiness with a thirst equal to the zeal of your own: till you delight in God for being good to all: you never enjoy the world. Till you more feel it than your private estate, and are more present in the hemisphere, considering the glories and the beauties there, than in your own house. Till you remember how lately you were made, and how wonderful it was when you came into it: and more rejoice in the palace of your glory, than if it had been made but today morning.

Yet further, you never enjoy the world aright, till you so love the beauty of enjoying it, that you are covetous and earnest to persuade others to enjoy it ... There is so much blindness and ingratitude and damned folly in it. The world is a mirror of infinite beauty, yet no man sees it. It is a Temple of Majesty, yet no man regards it. It is a region of Light and Peace, did man not disquiet it. It is the Paradise of God. It is more to man since he is fallen than it was before. It is the place of Angels and the Gate of Heaven. When Jacob waked out of his dream, he said "God is here and I wist it not. How awesome is this place! This is none other than the House of God, and the Gate of Heaven."

Thomas Traherne

Creator of the spirit, self-created,
    since all creation is only thought ungodded
by gradual matter, slowly separated
    from beauty that is for ever disembodied,

be near us when we build our city, indulge
    the builders' plan with starshine, turn the brick
with the courses of dawn, and let the sun divulge
    the secret of his gold arithmetic —

one among many. Be near us when we stumble
    through myriad shapes, wherewith, when thou art dim, age
muffles the streets of vision, and, when these crumble,
    let us remember of what they were the image.

Be near us when we fail, and, helpless, gaze on
    the turrets, and tall cathedrals, that we planned
to be the music of life in diapason,
    unravelling through silence, strand by strand.

When in the east the dawns we pass from wait red
    and angry, till our own creations fear us,
when love, that was the builder, turns to hatred
    of those for whom he builded, then be near us ...

Be near us always, but most of all when dawn
    breaks, and we see the City on the hill.

Humbert Wolfe

I went through the forest of time,
without a glimmer of light,
towards the unknown City.
I entered at night
the unknown City,
I was born for that moment.

Over the palaces not a single star,
architecture of darkness.
Blind, I went stumbling, feeling my way,
in search of my meaning.

There was only one of the hundred Dark Gates
that opened to swallow me
like a black pit —
the purest of them all, perhaps,
resembling despair ...

I entered the sealed City in darkness
and there were questions no longer.
Things simply were — without explanation ...
but the Presence was so tangible
that I could proceed leaning on silence,
having to guide me only a Wall
without beginning or end —

to discover at last the star
that lights up the night
of Jerusalem.

Sr Marie-Madeleine (Hélène Jung)

Al-Quds

Adam, tired, grown old, his strength weakened and eyesight dull, sorrow resting upon his heart. He sits alone in his vineyard, Abel is no longer, and Cain roams and wanders in the Land. With the sweat of his brow Adam eats bread. He looks at the world, and it is full of strife and contention. Each person does as he pleases. One dispossesses the other; another robs his neighbour. Adam calls out to his God with a great cry for peace and serenity to reside again, but his call is unanswered. And from the greatness of his anger and fury about a world which goes unrepaired, the old Adam bursts to his death and with a great blast is scattered to all the winds of the earth. The particles of his body fly for days searching for a resting place, and in the end land on a rock which would be called *Bayt al-Maqdis*. And from that time, every house built in Jerusalem shines with a yellowish-golden light from the holy skin of Adam our Father.

Slowly, slowly, with the building of the world, after the Flood, people started feeling a kind of magical strange attraction to the place where the rock and city surrounding it rested. All were pulled towards it with a kind of primeval emotion, neither fatherly nor motherly, and found themselves near the rock and Jerusalem, calling the place *Surrah* (navel). Adam, different from all his sons was not born of a mother and had no navel. His god, His name shall be blessed and exalted, created in him this navel power out of an abundance of love and yearning, and attraction is so powerful and unexplainable that the dove which Noah sent out chose the olive leaf from here, from the place which would be called the Mount of Olives, the Mount of Peace and Resurrection of the Dead.

Legend tells that after Adam left his father, Sakinat al-Quds came and dwelled in the caves of the place and in the crevices of its stones. It also relates that the prophet, the Lord's prayer be upon him, when coming to pray for the first time, turned towards Jerusalem, before the Ka'aba. And when he sought a partition to place in front of him, since his stick was not in his hands, he heard a voice tell him that the ram's horn from the Binding of Ismail was still on the rock of the navel in Jerusalem, and there was no need for an additional partition.

Not very long afterwards, The Prophet, the Lord's prayer be upon him, was called for a visit to heaven. Here, the winged horse, *al-Burak*, awaits him on the Holy Rock. He ascended to heaven; some say with Sakina on his shoulder. Many also make a connection between the footprint on the Rock and the leg of the Prophet, the Lord's prayer be upon him.

Afterwards, when Hisham ben Abd- al-Malek, came to Jerusalem to build the illustrious mosque on the Rock, he found the footprint and the horn of the Binding next to it. The horn hung in the mosque for many years, visible to every one, as evidence of man's love for his Creator and the mercy which God has in store for he who chooses paths of peace and righteousness.

The Mosque became famous in those days. Its dome was gold, its pillars marble and alabaster, and its gate was pure gold. Ninety nine white mules were required to carry the gold for the dome, and seven white mules — the gold for the gate. It would spread light in the heart of the believers, and banish darkness from their thoughts. But, in the passing of days, fewer visitors came to the house of the Lord, and it was distant from their heart. Evilness and wars intensified, and Sakina sits in Jerusalem weeping over the acts of men.

God's anger grew, and his fury knew no bounds. And on the second day of the week, the day on which Adam, Moses, and Muhammad, of blessed memory, gave up their souls, the heavens suddenly darkened, the sun covered her face, and the great trembling gripped the knees of the Land. The earth opened its mouth and swallowed up homes and their inhabitants. The ground surrounding the Mosque became cracked, and the bubbling wells of water around Jerusalem dried up. The righteous men of Jerusalem were summoned to prayer and entreaties.

The dome of the Rock begged for its life, its pillars and the layers underneath about to collapse. Before the foundation of the Mosque buckled under, Sakina flew with Burakian speed and grasped the golden ring at the center of the dome in her beak. She began to flap her wings wigh all her might to keep the building standing until the fury subsided. Much time passed until God heard the cries of Solomon bursting forth from the soot-covered stones of the Temple and the prayers of the righteous, and was appeased. Sakina's strength did not hold out. She strained, her veins and eyes bulging, and exactly at the moment the earth's convulsions subsided, she eruped into a great force and was scattered in tiny particles in every direction, just as it had happened to Adam. So, through her merit and the merit of her sacrifice the mosque was saved.

Who is Sakina? No one can say. Legend tells that she was one of the doves which Noah sent out, and after flying in the forests and above the seas, she chose freedom and serenity, beauty and holiness. She chose Jerusalem, al-Quds.

Roger Tavor

The Holy City, Bait-al-Makdis, is also known as Iliyâ and Al Balât. Among provincial towns none is larger than Jerusalem, and many capitals are, in fact, smaller. Neither the cold nor the heat is excessive here, and snow falls but rarely. The Kâdi Abu-l Kâsim, son of the Kâdi of the two Holy Cities of Makkah and Al Madinah, inquired of me once concerning the climate of Jerusalem. I answered: 'It is betwixt and between — neither very hot nor very cold.' Said he in reply: 'Just as is that of Paradise.' The buildings of the Holy City are of stone, and you will find nowhere finer or more solid construction. In no place will you meet with people more chaste. Provisions are most excellent here; the markets are clean, the Mosque is of the largest, and nowhere are Holy Places more numerous. The grapes are enormous, and there are no quinces to equal those of the Holy City. In Jerusalem are all manner of learned men and doctors, and for this reason the heart of every man of intelligence yearns towards her. All the year round, never are her streets empty of strangers. As to the saying that Jerusalem is the most illustrious of cities — is she not the one that unites the advantages of This World and those of the Next? He who is of the sons of This World, and yet is ardent in the matters of the Next, may find there a market for his wares; while he who would be of the men of the Next World, though his soul clings to the good things of This, he, too, may find them here! Further, Jerusalem is the pleasantest of places in the matter of climate, for the cold there does not injure, and the heat is not noxious. And as to her being the finest city, why, has any seen elsewhere buildings finer or cleaner, or a Mosque that is more beautiful? And as for the Holy City being the most productive of all places in good things, why, Allah — may He be exalted! — has gathered together here all the fruits of the lowlands, and of the plains, and of the hill country, even all those of the most opposite kinds: such as the orange and the almond, the date and the nut, the fig and the banana, besides milk in plenty, and honey and sugar. And as to the excellence of the City! why, is not this to be the place of marshalling on the Day of Judgment; where the gathering together and the appointment will take place? Verily Makkah and Al Madinah have their superiority by reason of the Ka'abah and the Prophet — the blessing of Allah be upon him and his family! — but, in truth, on the Day of Judgment both cities will come to Jerusalem, and the excellencies of them all will then be united. And as to Jerusalem being the most spacious of cities; why, since all created things are to assemble there, what place on the earth can be more extensive than this?

Muqaddasi

As for the view of Jerusalem from afar, filled with brilliance and beauty, it is one of the famous wonders. The most attractive view is that which one enjoys from the eastern side, from the Mount of Olives. Likewise from the south. But from the west and the north you can see only a small part of the city because of the mountains that conceal it. The cities of Jerusalem and Hebron are in effect situated on steep and rocky mountains where travel is difficult and round-about. The mountains that surround these two cities extend for nearly three days march, calculating with a pack animal, in width and breadth. Nonetheless, when God grants the pilgrim the favor of arriving at the solemn al-Aqsa shrine and the prayer station venerated by Abraham, he experiences an indescribable feeling of joy and well-being and forgets the pains and troubles he has endured. The poet Ibn Hujr improvised the following verses to precisely that point when he came on pilgrimage to Jerusalem:

'We came to Jerusalem with the hope of gaining pardon of our sins from a generous Master.

'For love of Him we have passed through Hell, but after Hell, there is nothing but Paradise.'

Mujir al-Din

The great mosque of Jerusalem, Al Masjid al Aksâ, the 'Further Mosque', derives its name from the traditional journey of the Prophet Muhammad to which allusion is made in the words of the Holy Qur'an:

Glory be to Him Who made His servant to go on a night from the Sacred Mosque to the remote Mosque of which We have blessed the precincts, so that We may show to him some of Our signs: surely He is the Hearing, the Seeing.

According to the received account the Prophet Muhammad was on this occasion mounted on the winged steed called Al Burâk — 'the Lightning' — and, with the angel Gabriel for escort, was carried from Makkah, first to Sinai, and then to Bethlehem, after which they came to Jerusalem. And when we reached Bait al Makdis, the Holy City, so runs the tradition, we came to the gate of the Mosque (which is the Haram Area), and here Jibrail caused me to dismount. And he tied up Al Burâk to a ring, to which the prophets of old had also tied their steeds. Entering the Haram Area by the gateway, afterwards known as the Gate of the Prophet, Muhammad and Gabriel went up to the Sacred Rock, which of old times had stood in the centre of Solomon's Temple; and in its neighbourhood meeting the company of the prophets, the Prophet Muhammad proceeded to perform his prayer-prostrations in the assembly of his predecessors in the prophetic office — Abraham, Moses, Jesus, and others of God's ancient apostles. From the Sacred Rock the Prophet Muhammad, accompanied by Gabriel, next ascended, by a ladder of light, up into heaven; and, in anticipation, was vouchsafed the sight of the delights of Paradise. Passing through the seven heavens, the Prophet Muhammad ultimately stood in the presence of Allah, from whom he received injunctions as to the prayers his followers were to perform. Thence, after a while, he decended again to earth; and, alighting at the foot of the ladder of light, stood again on the Sacred Rock at Jerusalem. The return journey homeward was made after the same fashion — on the back of the steed Al Burâk — and the Prophet reached Makkah again before the night had waned. Such, in outline, is the tradition of the Prophet's Night Journey, which especially sanctifies the Rock and the Haram Area in the sight of all true believers.

Guy Le Strange

In the eastern wall of the Haram area there is a great gateway so skillfully built of squared stones that one might almost say that the whole was carved out of a single block. Its height is fifty ells and its width thirty, and it is sculpted and ornamented throughout. There are ten beautiful doors in this gateway (set so close) that between any two of them there is not the space of a foot. The doors are all most skillfully wrought in iron and Damascus brass work, set in with bolts and rings. They say that this gateway was constructed by Solomon, son of David — peace be upon him — to please his father. When you enter this gateway facing east there are on your right hand two great doors. One of them is called the Gate of Mercy and the other the Gate of Repentance, and they say of this last that it is the gate where God — may He be exalted and glorified — accepted the repentance of David — upon whom be peace.

Nasir-i Khusraw

The Court (of the Haram Area) is paved in all parts; In the centre of the Platform is the Dome of the Rock ... At the dawn, when the light of the sun first strikes on the Cupola, and the drum reflects his rays, then is this edifice a marvellous sight to behold, and one such that in all Islam I have never seen the equal.

Muqaddasi

Each day fifty and two persons were employed to pound and grind down saffron, working by night also, and leavening it with musk and ambergris, and rose-water of the Jûri rose. At early dawn the servants appointed entered the Bath of Sulaimân ibn 'Abd al Malik, where they washed and purified themselves before proceeding to the Treasure Chamber (al Khazânah), in which was kept the (yellow perfume of saffron called) Khulûk. And, before leaving the Treasure Chamber, they changed all their clothes, putting on new garments, made of the stuffs of Marv and Herat, also shawls (of the striped cloths of Yaman), called 'Asb; and, taking jewelled girdles, they girt these about their waists. Then, bearing the jars of the Khulûk in their hands, they went forth and anointed therewith the stone of the Rock, even as far as they could reach up to with their hands, spreading the perfume all over the same. And for the part beyond that which they could reach, having first washed their feet, they attained thereto by walking on the Rock itself, anointing all that remained thereof; and by this the jars of the Khulûk were completely emptied. Then they brought censers of gold and silver, filled with aloes wood of Kimâr (in Java), and the incense called Nadd, compounded with musk and ambergris; and, letting down the curtains between the columns, they swung to and fro the censers, until the incense did rise into all the space between the columns and the Dome above, by reason of the quantity thereof. Which done, and the curtains again drawn up, the censers were carried outside the building, whereby the sweet smell went abroad, even to the entrance of the market beyond (the Haram area), so that all who passed therein could scent the perfume. After this the censers were extinguished. Proclamation then was made by criers from before the screen: 'The Sakhrah, verily, is open for the people, and he who would pray therein, let him come.' And the people would hasten to come and make their prayer in the Sakhrah, the most of them performing two Rika'ahs (or prayer prostrations), while some few acquitted themselves of four. And he who had thus said his prayers, when he had gone forth again, (friends) would perceive on him the perfume of the incense, and say: 'Such an one hath been in the Sakhrah.' (After the prayer-time was over, the servants) washed off with water the marks left by the peoples' feet, cleaning everywhere with green myrtle (brooms), and drying with cloths. Then the gates were closed, and for guarding each were appointed ten chamberlains, since none might enter the Sakhrah — except the servants thereof — on other days than the Monday and the Friday.

On the authority of Abu Bakr ibn al Hârith, it is reported that, during the Khalifate of 'Abd al Malik, the Sakhrah was entirely lighted with (oil of) the Midian Bân (the Tamarisk, or Myrobalan) tree, and oil of Jasmin, of a lead colour. (And this, says Abu Bakr, was of so sweet a perfume, that) the chamberlains were wont to say to him: 'O Abu Bakr, pass us the lamps that we may put oil on ourselves therefrom, and perfume our clothes'; and so he used to do, to gratify them. Such are the matters relating to the days of the Khalifate of 'Abd al Malik.

(Muthir al-Ghiram)

Allah says of Jerusalem
  beneath you I placed all the sweet waters which
  flow from the mountain tops
                              Ka'b al-Ahbar

The roofs of all the buildings in the Haram Area are covered with lead. Below the ground-level are numerous tanks and water-cisterns hewn out of the rock, for the Noble Sanctuary rests everywhere on a foundation of live rock. There are so many of these cisterns that however much rain falls, no water flows away to waste, but all is caught in the tanks, whence the people come to draw it. They have constructed leaden conduits for carrying down the water, and the rock cisterns lie below these, with covered passages leading down thereto, through which the conduits pass to the tanks, whereby any loss of water is saved, and impurities are kept therefrom.

At a distance of three leagues from the Holy City, I saw a great water-tank (at Solomon's Pools), whereinto pour all the streams that flow down from the hills. From thence they have brought an aqueduct that comes out into the Noble Sanctuary. Of all parts of the Holy City this is where water is most plentiful. But in every house also, there is a cistern for collecting the rain-water — for other than this water there is none — and each must store the rain which falls upon his roof. The water used in the hot baths and other places is solely from the storage of the rains. The tanks that are below the Haram Area never need to be repaired, for they are cut in the live rock. Any place where there may have been originally a fissure or a leakage, has been so solidly built up that the tanks never fall out of order. It is said that these cisterns were constructed by Solomon — peace be upon him! The roofing of them is like that of a baker's oven (*tannûr*). Each opening is covered with a stone, as at a well-mouth, in order that nothing may fall therein. The water of the Holy City is sweeter than the water of any other place, and purer; and even when no rain falls for two or three days the conduits still run with water, for though the sky be clear, and there be no trace of clouds, the dew causes drops to fall.

Nasir-i Khusraw

Allah, may He be praised and exalted, said of Jerusalem:
You are My Garden of Eden

Ka'b al-Ahbar

If I Forget Thee

Long, long ago — two brothers inherited their father's great estate. It had fields, orchards, vineyards. Even a towering hill at its centre. They worked hard and well and they prospered. In the evening they returned to their own homes — discreetly built at opposite ends of the farm. Truly, they loved and respected each other.

One night — when the year's harvest had been completed, the abundant produce evenly divided and carefully stored in their two barns — the brothers sat in their homes but neither of them could sleep.

The older one — as he listened to the deep and contented breathing of his wife and children — thought: "How fortunate and blessed I am — while my brother lives all alone. The only things he has to enjoy is the produce of our land. Why not let him a little more. I can so easily slip a little extra into his barn!" Quickly, he loaded his cart with the choicest of his produce and began to pull it in the direction of his brother's home.

The younger brother was also deep in thought: "Surely I have no need for all that is in my barn! My brother has so many more mouths to feed and would not dream of asking for a larger share. Why not let him a little more ..." And he, too, loaded his cart with the finest of his produce and as quickly as he could pulled the heavy load in the direction of his brother's home.

The moon was full and the night still. It was hard to get the cart up the hill — but the descent would be easier — and how much sweeter the sleep afterwards. So each of them was thinking as they reached the crest of the hill. And there — as if drawn by unseen threads of love — the two brothers came a little panting face to face with each other. At once each understood the purpose of the other. Without a word they embraced and for a long time they held one another. This harmony was complete and their love generous and giving.

And it was on that very spot — many generations later — after his father David bought that hill and the surrounding lands and named it *Yerushalaim* — it was there that Solomon laid the foundation of the Temple to the glory of the God of Israel and left a vision and a model of *shalom* for the Family of Israel.

There men and women, Kings and priests, indeed all who loved and revered the name of God brought their offerings — of heart, spirit and mind as well as the produce of their land and hands — in gratitude and hope as well as in anxiety and distress. And, in time, there too came the enemies of Israel. But the vision of building the Kingdom of God on earth could not be eradicated.

Those first exiles — two-and-a-half millennia ago — newly arrived in Babylonea — as soon as they took their bearings they turned towards Jerusalem. "Cheer up — and cheer us up, too," said their captors. Life has to go on. The Jews knew and understood this as well. Their own prophet — Jeremiah — sent just that message before the City finally fell. "Build houses and live in them," he urged. "Plant vineyards and eat the fruit of them. Get husbands for your daughters and wives for your sons. And pray for the welfare of your city — because in its welfare is your welfare ..."

So they would go on — living and building — but they made a holy oath there and then. That they would also live for Jerusalem as well. And build bits of Jerusalem in everything they would build ... The holy ark of every synagogue faces Jerusalem and wherever Jews rise in collective prayer their voices rise up but are also directed towards Jerusalem. In every Jewish home there is a small plaque — some ornate, some simple and stark — fixed to that wall which faces Jerusalem. The daily prayers recall Jerusalem. The grace after every meal pleads for the restoration of Jerusalem. Sabbath and festival afternoons echo the promise: "And the Redeemer shall come to Zion ..."

At every wedding a glass is broken — a reminder of the fall of Jerusalem — and coupled with a prayer that one day something of the sound of joy born of love and fulfillment will echo in the very streets of Jerusalem.

Has there ever been a people to keep such faith with a pledge to remember? And to recall not only the devastation — but also to cherish the vision of a return, of restoration and rebuilding? Even now — when her children have returned and can celebrate her beauty — the prayers have not ceased nor is the vision dimmed. Jerusalem is not yet that City of God which can proclaim the Oneness of God, the unity of humanity and those harmonies promised by *Shalom*.

But where those brothers first met — brothers and sisters can meet again. And until that happens hearts and eyes will turn to Jerusalem. David understood this when he sang — "How good and how pleasant it is when brothers meet in unity!" — and so will his descendants who will not give up on the vision ...

Rabbi Hugo Gryn

Your stones I shall polish into a mirror
For in them is my yearning.
Pines' loftiness and their hearts' resin.

In dawns' topazes
I shall store
The reflection of your day
Rising early on the city wall
Like a stream of light
On a slope of flint
In a bronze mortar sheath.

Your stones I shall polish until my dreams course in you
Like a flow smashing your rocks —
Your yearning, wanderer.

David Rokeah

Zion, will you not ask after your imprisoned ones,
The remnant of your flocks, who seek your peace?
From west and east, and north and south,
From far and near, take greetings, from all sides,
And peace from the captive of desire, whose tears fall
Like Hermon's dew, while he longs to shed them on
     your hills.
I am a jackal mourning your affliction, and when I
     dream
Of the return of your captives I am a lyre accompanying
     your songs.

Who will make me wings, so I can fly away
And take my broken heart to your mountain clefts?
Let me fall prostrate upon your land, treasure
Your stones, and fondle your fine dust.

The air of your land is the soul's very life, your clouds
     of dust
Flowing myrrh, and liquid honey your streams.
It would soothe my soul to walk naked and barefoot
Upon the desolate ruins that were once your sanctuary,
On the place of your ark, now concealed, and the spot
In the holy of holies where your cherubim dwelt.

Zion, beauty's perfection, who have enwrapped yourself
     in love and grace,
The souls of your companions are bound to you.
They delight in your peace, mourn
Your desolation, bewail your destruction.
From the pit of captivity they aspire towards you,
Bow, each in his place, towards your gates.
They are the flocks of your people, exiled and scattered
Through hill and valley, and yet they remember your
     folds.
They cling to your robes, and strive
To climb up and clasp your palms' top branches...

Judah ha-Levi

If I forget thee, Jerusalem,
Then let my right be forgotten.
Let my right be forgotten, and my left remember.
Let my left remember, and your right close
And your mouth open near the gate.

I shall remember Jerusalem
And forget the forest — my love will remember,
Will open her hair, will close my window,
Will forget my right,
Will forget my left.

If the west wind does not come
I'll never forgive the walls,
Or the sea, or myself.
Should my right forget,
My left shall forgive,
I shall forget all water,
I shall forget my mother.

If I forget thee, Jerusalem,
Let my blood be forgotten.
I shall touch your forehead,
Forget my own,
My voice change
For the second and last time
To the most terrible of voices —
Or silence.

Yehuda Amichai

The Torah, my children, what is it?
A treasure-filled with gold and precious stones.
To penetrate it, you need a key. I shall impart
one to you; use it well. The key, my children, is what?
The Alphabet. So then, repeat after me, with me, in full
voice, louder: aleph, beit, gimmel …

Elie Wiesel

There had been multitudes, yea, multitudes, O God —
So many lively ones, and so many gallant,
So stately and so bearded, and so crowned with talent —
Whose language was astonishing, and nobly odd.

From under every rooftop with its gabled slopes
Such curious songs, and such haughty ones they'd sing,
Of the splendid peacock and Elimelekh the King,
With biblical cymbals, and the appropriate tropes.

But high above their heads, only the sun could see
The raw attack, the cold knife of the murderer
As he descended on them in a violent stir,
And what a lot there was of savage butchery …

Now they are melted, they are what violence can remember
Two or three trees left standing amid the fallen timber.

Mani Leyb

The rock decays
From which I spring
To sing my songs of God …
Headlong I rush from the way
And murmur deep within,
Seaward, distant, and alone
Over the wailingstones.

I have flowed so far away
From the must, the ferment,
Of my blood.
And still, still the echo
In me,
When to the East, awesomely,
The decaying rock of bone,
My people,
Cries out to God.

Else Lasker-Schüler

O Lord, how long shall I cry
and thou wilt not hear!
I cry out unto thee of violence,
and thou wilt not save

And the Lord answered me:
Write the vision, and make it plain upon tablets
that he may run who reads it
For still the vision awaits its time;
it hastens to the end — it will not lie

Habakkuk

Fear not, for I am with thee; I will bring thy seed
from the east, and gather thee from the west;
I will say to the north, Give up; and to the south,
Keep not back: bring my sons from far and my daughters
from the end of the earth

(Isaiah 43)

Wedge me into the fissure with each fallen stone.
Hammer me till I grow strong.
Perhaps I shall appease my land and atone
For the people's sin: the ruins unmended so long.

To be one of the stones of my city is all my desire.
Where my bones knitted in the wall, how glad I would be.
Is my body less than my soul, that through water and fire
Stayed by the people, who shrieked or went silently?

With the stones of Jerusalem wedge me into the wall.
Clothe me in mortar, and from
The very depths of the stones my bones shall call
Till the Messiah come.

Yehuda Karni

Go, ship, and make for the land
Which contains the Shechinah's abode.
Hasten your flight, moved forward by God's hand.
Bind your wing to the wings of the morning breeze,
For those borne along by the wind in your sails,
For the hearts torn into a thousand pieces.

Judah ha-Levi

Eat and drink
Eat   and drink because
tomorrow we're not going to die   because
we're going to live   because
we're going to go through the whole twilit city
from end to end
that Hebrew city between the veiled hills because
you stand revealed
with me by your side,
my beautiful bridegroom:
we sun-watchers lie down in the   field
we'll be. And until the sun shines
on the wall again we'll lie down again mouth   to mouth
and anyone who's seen it all and said nothing
will see   again
under the tree's spreading boughs
how love is torn
you and I and the canopies overhead
are seven,
my beautiful bridegroom.

Abba Kovner

I do not hold a mirage in my hand —
my shirt's in my hand. The plain filled
with my wheat. All of it. Soaked by dew
flat at my feet. Its beauty
turns each image pale. The returning heron
and the apple garden. Sun
plucks at my shoulders like my daughter's
            fingers
And this day
recalling soon
the smell of the harvest:
this morning (I say to myself)
even in the burned forest the bird
has come back to sing.

Abba Kovner

'From the beginning of His creation of the world, the Holy, blessed be He, has chiefly concerned Himself with planting, as it is said "And God the Lord planted a garden in Eden." So too you, when you come into the land, are to concern yourselves chiefly with planting. If your hand is busy with planting and they say to you "Messiah is come!", finish your planting first and then go out and receive Him.'

(the Midrash)

These Lights We now Kindle

And to Jerusalem your city in mercy you shall return
and dwell there as you desired

And build and build and build
Her, her, her …

He therefore decided to revive the festival of the Maccabees for his children, and to plant in their young souls a feeling of relationship to the past of their people. As he held aloft the nine-branched candlestick he suddenly recalled, in a strange rush of feeling, his own childhood, and the celebration of the festival in his father's house. He looked at the antique symbol, the prototype of which had so obviously been a tree, and asked himself "whether it was possible to bring new life into his petrified menorah form, and to water its roots again as if it were really a tree." And thus the first evening of the Hanukkah festival passed.

The first candle was lit, and the story of the origin of the festival recited: the miraculous origin of the undying lamp, the saga of the return from Babylon, of the Second Temple and of the Maccabees. Our friend related to his children all that he knew. It was not much, but it was enough for them. When he lit the second candle, it was the children who recited the story to him, and as he heard it from their lips it seemed not only beautiful, but quite new. And from then on he looked forward joyfully to the coming of each evening, always brighter than the evening before. Candle stood by candle in the menorah, and by their light, father and children dreamed their dreams. In the end it all grew into something more than he had sought to tell them, for it had risen beyond their understanding ...

Amid these meditations the week passed. The eighth day came, and now the *shammash*, the servant among the candles, which until then had been used only for the kindling of the others, burned together with them. A great light streamed out from the menorah. The eyes of the children flashed, but what our good friend saw was the kindling of the light of the nation. First one candle, and dimness all around it, so that the candle was sad and lonely. Then a companion was added to it. Then a third, and a fourth. The darkness is compelled to retreat. The first candles are lit among the young and the poor, and gradually they are joined by all those who love truth and beauty and justice and freedom. When all the candles burn there is admiration and rejoicing for the work that has been done. And there is no office more beneficent and creative than that of a Servant of Light.

Theodor Herzl

'Just as our fathers founded new ways of serving, each a new service according to his character: one the service of love, the other that of stern justice, the third that of beauty, so each one of us in his own way shall devise something new in the light of teachings and of service, and do what has not yet been done.'

Every person born into this world represents something new, something that never existed before, something original and unique.

Martin Buber

Jerusalem! Cry of the hungry heart, oblivion's
garden beyond the hills when refugees fled the storm —
Silence you are, submission and rebellion.
Because of you, heart shudders, the griefs swarm.

By green of your earth I swear and by your sunlight.
I inherit the desolation that remains.
I stand like a tree in stone, by you held spellbound —
soul woven with soul, my root in your dry veins.

I love what survives in you as in cold lava,
the rejoicing sound of ancient days,
echoing still from your white rocks of silence.

But with your holiness is now my strife,
and I have come to smash rocks into clods.
Dead splendour rests on furrows of new life.

Jacob Fichman

Motke

For wisdom will enter your heart,
and knowledge will be pleasant to your soul.

And I took root among an honoured people,
   in the portion of the Lord, in his inheritance.
Like a cedar on Lebanon I grew tall,
   like a cypress on Mount Hermon.
Like a terebinth I spread out my branches,
   and my branches are full of glory and grace.
Like a vine I caused loveliness to bud,
   and my blossoms became glorious and abundant fruit.
Come to me, you who desire me,
   and you will eat your fill of my produce,
for to think of me is sweeter than honey,
   and to possess me is better than honey in the comb.

The British Academy sends its most cordial good wishes on the great occasion of the opening of the Hebrew University of Jerusalem — an event fraught with happiest augury for the progress of human knowledge and with historic significance as acclaiming the holy City among the seats of modern learning and research...

May the Hebrew University of Jerusalem add new lustre to the enduring fame and immemorial glory of the sacred City inestimably endeared to mankind! Fostered by a succession of gifted teachers, may learning and arts of peace grow from strength to strength and flourish in the University — a Foundation of Peace in the City of Peace.

In fraternal comradeship with scholars and scientists throughout the world may the Hebrew University of Jerusalem advance the welfare of the human race, and above all through Knowledge, help forward the realiz-ation of the Psalmists praise of all transcending Wisdom! —

(The British Academy represented by
The Earl of Balfour, President of the Academy)

We are all deeply conscious that Israel has at this moment lit on the Mount of Olives the first light of the Dedication of his spiritual life. Today it will be heralded to all Israel in all parts of the world, that the corner-stone of Upper Jerusalem has been laid. For this strange nation, known as Israel, despite all the storms which for two thousand years have swept over it to destroy it and uproot it — this nation, I say, has pledged its loyalty to the Kingdom of the Mind and Spirit for ever. In this Kingdom, Israel is like a fresh young tree with strong roots; Israel has planted his feet on this soil and will not stir from here. Numberless years of accursed exile have not changed his spirit; countless years of corruptive poverty have not undermined his fundamental character. Forced by necessity to forego the comforts of daily life for the external life of the spirit, he has learned in the days of his downtrodden poverty to subordinate his physical to his spiritual needs, to subject his material wants to the demands of the spirit. Within this kingdom the Jewish Nation has created its chief possessions and institutions, which have kept it alive, despite its poverty, through two thousand years of wandering, have preserved its inner freedom within the shell of its outer bondage, and have preserved us for this great day, the day of the inauguration of the University of Mount Scopus ...

There is an ancient Jewish legend which tells us that at the time of our redemption, all the Jewish synagogues and schools in the Diaspora, together with their foundations would be lifted up and would be transferred to Palestine. Naturally, this legend cannot be realised in full. The institution of Torah and learning which has been established on Mount Scopus, will be quite different in building material, in content, and in form from the old schools. But among the ruins of those sacred institutions there still remain perfect slabs of stone, hewn stones which can be used as foundation stones for our new institution. May we have the wisdom to raise the learning and science which shall come forth from this institution to that moral height to which our forefathers raised the Torah ...

Knowing that true wisdom learns from all people we shall open wide the gates and windows of this institution in all directions to admit all the good and sublime which has ever been and is being created by the mind of man. Yet not being novices in the Kingdom of the Mind and Spirit, we feel that while learning from others we also have something to contribute. And I am confident that the same moral principles, which have been laid down as the fundamental principles of our schools, shall become the possession of all humanity.

Thousands of our young men and women, listening to the inner promptings of their hearts, stream from the four corners of the world to this country to rescue it from its present state of desolation and ruin, prepared to give to their country their best energies and their youth. They plough among the rocks, drain the swamps, and cut roads with song and rejoicing. These young people have learnt to exalt simple, rough toil to the sacredness of a religion. We must light this holy fire within the walls of the institution which has now been opened on Mount Scopus. Let those youths build the Earthly Jerusalem with fire and let them who work within these walls build the Heavenly Jerusalem with fire, and between them let them build our House of Life.

Hayyim Nahman Bialik

O, from your sweet mouth
I learned too much of bliss!
Already I feel Gabriel's lips
Burning on my breast . . .
And the night-cloud drinks
My deep dream of cedars.
O, how your life beckons me!
And I dissolve
With blossoming heartbreak
And I drift away in the universe
Into time,
To forever,
And my soul burns away in the evening colors
Of Jerusalem.

Else Lasker-Schüler

The love of the Jew for the Hebrew language, popularly called 'the sacred tongue,' is one of the most precious national possessions of the Jewish people. This love is woven, like a golden thread, throughout Jewish history, for the Jew knows that 'the sacred tongue' is the eternal tongue of his people. One generation passeth away and another generation cometh; and the Hebrew language abideth forever. Exile may end and redemption come and the root-language of the land of Israel stands firm.

'The universe was created by means of the holy tongue' — thus spoke the Jewish sages because to them the universe was revealed in Hebrew. They felt, and many feel with them today, that through the Hebrew language the Jewish national and cultural character is most truly revealed. There live in this language historic Jewish concepts and Hebrew expressions that are peculiar and unique and find their like in no other language. There are words, phrases and verses whose roots go so deep that they touch the limits of time and thus can have their comparison in no other tongue. Every word bears the scent of ancient eras and has the savor of old wines that stir up longings that transcend the boundaries of language.

Therefore the man who speaks or writes such a language becomes a partner with the great of distant epochs and enters a mystical enclosure with those noblemen of spirit who lived most richly and he draws sustenance from their fountain. He feels that a great and majestic hand casts him — in the phrase of Hayyim Nahman Bialik — into 'an unexplored height, an unknown remoteness.'

For it was through the Hebrew language that the God of Israel revealed Himself ... and the Torah was given to Israel.

All the statutes and ordinances of the Torah, by which the Jewish people has lived for thousands of years, were written in Hebrew. Similarly, the Hebrew language has been warp and woof of the Jewish fabric from the conquest of Canaan, to the destruction of the first Temple and the Babylonian captivity; from the first King to the last Prophet; from the return from Babylonian exile to the destruction of the second Temple. Hebrew has been branch and root of the Jewish creations of the spirit from Ezra and the men of the Great Synagogue to the days of the writing of the Mishnah and the Gemara; from the Halakhic literature to the literature of mysticism; from the Gaonic literature and that of the Middle Ages through the Kabbalah and Hassidism and the Haskalah — up to our own time, to the restoration of the Jewish State.

The entire Jewish approach to life, in which are united the earthly and the heavenly, the material and the spiritual, finds full and exact expression in the Hebrew language. Abstract and lofty concepts are blended together with the concrete and simple. Symbolic images of the completely incorporeal divine dwell honorably side by side with very human descriptions, converting the spirit into matter and the godly into human. The anthropomorphic element is characteristic of the Bible and, therefore, of Hebrew.

Yes, generations come and generations go, languages and cultures enter the world and pass on, but the Hebrew tongue remains, it stands forever. Actually, the word 'stands' is inaccurate, for Hebrew moves; it is alive, constantly developing and rejuvenating itself with new vitality.

This is an inner vitality, one of the soul, for Hebrew has lived within the Jewish people, in all periods and ages, in all lands and in all its exiles. In Babylonia and Persia, in Greece and Egypt, in Spain and Africa, in Germany and Poland, in Italy and France, in Lithuania and Rumania and in North and South America, the Hebrew language, like a good and faithful angel, accompanied the people it loved.

In every age and in every land, there arose redeemers for Hebrew in the shape of poets and scholars and codifiers and grammarians. They played upon the harp of the language so that the chords of the people vibrated ... Love for a language is one of the highest rungs in the ladder of human culture ...

But it is not only the poet, the author, the philosopher or the philologist who finds in the Hebrew language a matter of life and of creativity. The ordinary Hebraist too, the earnest reader, the lover of Hebrew sees in it a precious gift given him by the God of the Hebrews to be the object of his love. He derives joy from every new creation in Hebrew not only for its own intrinsic worth, but also because of its linguistic value. Hebraists are grammarians and linguistic stylists *par excellence.* And for them 'the joy of language' is akin to 'the joy of the Sabbath' to the traditional Jew.

It is because of the Jew's great and enduring love for the Hebrew language that there has come to pass the great marvel of the renaissance of the Hebrew language in our generation. And through this revival has come, in part, the rebirth of the Jewish State, for it was the Hebrew language that was a powerful force in the revival and redemption both of the people and of the land.

It was the Hebrew language that, through all the vagaries of time, was the fortress of strength in which the Jew, cleaving to the rock whence he was hewn, entrenched himself. Through the language of the prayers and hymns, the lamentations and penitential psalms, his heart would cleave not only to his Father in heaven but also to his desolate land for which he yearned and to whose redemption he looked forward. This land would live in his heart through the poetic descriptions of the Bible that were included in the prayer book and that became the daily bread of the Jew...

All of these desires and yearnings formed such an integral part of the Hebrew language that it became impossible to distinguish between the two. It is possible to say without exaggeration that the essence of the chant of the prayers in their gentle and soulful language would quiet the sighing of the heart and calm the storm of longing. Thus the uttering of the Hebrew words of the prayers was not only a means to an end but an end in itself in no small measure. In itself it became a great individual and national achievement.

Is it any wonder then, that with the Haskalah period, the period of enlightenment, and after it, the age of the renaissance, the Hebrew language became so precious and powerful an instrument for revival and redemption? All of modern Hebrew literature was born and grew with this concept of the redemption of the people and the land.

Now that Israel has been established, great days lie in store for the Hebrew language, days of creativity and development, the like of which has not been experienced in many generations.

Thus a generation goeth and a generation cometh, a language goeth and a language cometh, exile goeth and redemption cometh — and the Hebrew language endureth forever.

Menachem Ribalow

I wander through my city's nights
breathing emptied lanes
I sit in parks on sudden benches
the streetlights blooming after midnight
silence dripping from the pines
it's then I'll hear my city's breath
my city walking
garbed in stone.

Miriam Tal

Under these historic skies
I am older than Abraham and his stars,
and I am the young father of the children
playing among pink trees.

On Alharizi Street, on a violet afternoon,
such an hour of grace
gazes out of an arched frame
as sometimes whispered to the prophet
weary of fires,
who dreamed of a village
cool among the stars.

Gabriel Preil

This windmill never ground flour
It ground holy air and Bialik's
Birds of longing, it ground
Words and ground time, it ground
Rain and even shells
But it never ground flour.

Now it's discovered us,
And grinds our lives day by day
Making out of us the flour of peace
Making out of us the bread of peace
For the generation to come.

Yehuda Amichai

No limits are set to the ascent of man, and to
each and everyone the highest stands open. Here
it is only your personal choice that decides.

In the days to come,
The Mount of the Lord's House
Shall stand firm above the mountains
And tower above the hills;
And all the nations shall gaze on it with joy.
And the many people shall go and say:
'Come …'
And they shall beat their swords into plowshares
And their spears into pruning hooks:
Nation shall not take up
Sword against nation;
They shall never again know war.

(Isaiah 2)

142

Motke

I am, says God, Master of the Three Virtues.

Faith is a faithful wife.
Charity is an ardent mother.
But hope is a tiny girl ...

My little hope is she
who goes to sleep every night,
in that child's crib of hers,
after having said her prayers properly,
and who every morning wakes up and rises
and says her prayers with a new look in her eyes ...

Faith is a great tree ...
And my little hope is nothing but that little earnest of a bud ...
And when one sees the tree ...
When one sees such strength and such roughness, the tender little
bud no longer seems to be anything at all ...

And yet it is from that bud that everything comes. Without a bud
that once appeared, the tree would not exist. Without those thousands
of buds that come out ... nothing would last, the tree would not last
and would not keep its place as a tree (that place must be kept),
without that sap which rises and weeps ... without those thousand of
buds that begin to grow tenderly at the armpits of the hard limbs.

Every place must be kept. All life comes from tenderness. All life
comes from that tender, delicate bud and from that sap that weeps, and

from the cotton-wool and the down of that delicate white bud that is
clad, that is warmly, that is tenderly protected by the tuft of the
fleece of a vegetable wool, the wool of a tree.
In that cotton like tuft lies the secret of all life. The rough
bark looks like a cuirass in comparison with that tender bud.
But the rough bark is nothing but a hardened bud, a bud grown old.
And that is why the tender bud always pierces through, always
springs up from under the rough bark.
The toughest warrior was once upon a time a tender child,
a child fed on milk …

Now I tell you, says God, that without that budding, without
those thousands of buds, without that one little budding of hope,
which obviously anyone can break off, without that tender, cotton-
like bud, which the first man who comes along can snapp off with his
nail, the whole of my creation would be nothing but dead wood …

I am, says God, the Lord of virtues.
Faith is the sanctuary lamp
That burns forever.
Charity is that big, beautiful log fire
That you light in your hearth …
But my hope is the bloom, and the fruit, and the leaf and the
limb,
And the twig, and the shoot, and the seed, and the bud.
Hope is the shoot, and the bud of the bloom
Of eternity itself

Charles Peguy

The Healing of Peace

For behold! I am creating a new heaven and a new earth ... For I shall create Jerusalem as a joy, and her people as a delight. And I will rejoice in Jerusalem and delight in her people.
Never again shall be heard there the sounds of weeping and wailing ...
In all My sacred mount nothing evil or vile shall be done

(Isaiah 65)

He who brings about peace is called
the companion of God in the work of creation

Blue waterfalls flowing downwards
heavenly city floats naked
how blind we were of hearing
deaf of seeing
prisoners of false longings
striving towards the heights
step by step
each one and his own steps
ascending
until the end.

In the depths an emptied heaven
our increasing isolation whispers to you
a Song of Ascents.

Raphael Davara

1

I lie like a stone on the hill,
indifferent and silent
in the withered, sun-seared grass.
Pale skies touch rock.
Where does the yellow-winged butterfly come from?
A stone among stones, I do not know
the ancientness of my life
or who will yet come
and with a kick
send me rolling down the slope.

Perhaps it is beauty frozen forever,
perhaps eternity
moving slowly.
Perhaps it is
a dream of death,
or a dream
of the one love.

I lie like a stone on the hill
in thorn and thistle,
where a road below slides to the city.
Soon the wind that blesses all things
will come, to caress the pine crests
and the dumb stones.

2

All the things
outside love
come to me now:
this landscape with its old man's understanding
begging to live
one more year, one more year,
one generation more,
one more eternity.

To bring forth thorns endlessly,
to rock dead stones
like children in their cradles
before they sleep.
To silence ancient memories,
one more one more
one more.

How strong the lust for life
in those about to die.
How terrible the longing
and how vain:
to live, to live
one more year, one more year,
one generation more,
one more eternity.

3

How could a joyous bird
lose itself in these hills?
With a love song in her throat,
her little heart throbbing with gladness,
the promises of young ones soon in the nest,
her wings hymning love.
But suddenly before her
from the blue height
unrolls
a wasteland
stoned to death.

Save her,
save her,
save her
from seeing
the corpse of every love,
the grave of every joy.

In her blue
altitudes
singing love,
solitary
she hangs,
without reaching
the death
that confronts her.

4

How can one bird alone
hold up the whole sky
over the waste
with fragile wings?
The sky is boundless and blue,
but it is uplifted by wings,
sustained by the song of a bird.

Thus did my heart sustain my love.
It was boundless and blue,
above all altitudes —
above wasteland
mounds of ruins
gulfs of grief.

Until the song in my breast grew silent,
its strength failed,
and turning to stone,
it fell.

My mute, wounded love —
how can one bird alone
hold up the whole sky?

Leah Goldberg

151

Guard me, Oh God, from hating man my brother,
Guard me from recalling what, from my early youth, to me he did.
When all the stars in my sky are quenched, within me my soul's
   voice grows mute
When I am overcome by disaster, let me not lay bare his guilt.

For he is my hidden dwelling-place, in him am I reflected again.
Like a wayfarer from the planets, beholding his face in a pool.
What use is all my struggle, to whom shall I wail out the pain
If hollow, blemished is my distant night's moon?

When the gates are locked, darkness over the city reclining.
And emptied of love, rejected, I am bound to my rock:
Permit me to see in him a spark, only a spark still shining.
That I may know that in myself, in me, all is not yet snuffed out.

                                      Shin Shalom

Ishmael, my brother,
How long shall we fight each other?

My brother from times bygone,
My brother — Hagar's son,
My brother, the wandering one.

One angel was sent to us both,
One angel watched over our growth —
There in the wilderness, death threatening through thirst,
I a sacrifice on the altar, Sarah's first.

Ismael, my brother, hear my plea:
It was the angel who tied thee to me ...

Time is running out, put hatred to sleep.
Shoulder to shoulder, let's water our sheep.

                                        Shin Shalom

Isaac,
from the day I came into the world I knew
you would be coming as well, knew
that when I went into the desert with Hagar, my mother,
I would have for drink, water from a single flask;
for food, dry crusts of bread;
for shelter, a thorny desert bush —
while you would be sitting at ease in the shade of vine —
having as offering a lamb from your stock,
but I, only the stingy waters of a spring.
You are the son of Sarah's jealousy,
I the mocking son of a bondwoman shedding tears.
You became a shepherd, I an archer,
a son of the wilderness.
Our father turned me away lest I share his heritage;
yet here were two nations struggling
in Rebecca's womb.
You will never be at one with yourself —
till Esau and Jacob
and you and I are one.
Take me with you to sit in a fig tree's shade and I
shall cast away my bow.
Together we shall drink from the Paran spring
and our flocks drink too.

Nidaa Khouri

Into my lap a great star will fall ...
We would waken the night,

And pray in tongues
Carved like harps.

We would be reconciled with the night —
So much of God overflows.

Our hearts are children
Who, weary-sweet, would rest.

Our lips would kiss each other,
What do you fear?

Does my heart not verge on yours —
My cheeks are still stained red with your blood.

We would be reconciled with the night,
If we embrace, we shall not die.

Into my lap a great star will fall.

Else Lasker-Schüler

All ordinary things wait for the calm rising anxious and slow from people whose lives were spent in a blazing storm.

All ordinary things are very patient, their appearance takes on a sad grandeur as twilight falls with the gold day at the feet of the wanderer alone on an empty plain. And they are so beautiful you forget everything. It's like spring in the heart of a boy sitting on the bank of a lake. And all the bells ringing around you pouring out stream after stream though you can't see stone towers or turrets anywhere.

All ordinary things lie safe and dreamy like flocks of sheep. Like biblical wells on ancient crossroads. Like eternal walls where gods were revealed on both sides when lightning lit their antiquity when rain rinsed their gray faces generation after generation. That also remember their sorrow when the first rain caused nothing on their backs.

All ordinary things keep stroking consoling hands hidden inside and sounds of silence that soothe the eyes the forehead the face of a man weathered by time, come back from the heart of the storm.

And the ordinary things put him together and cover him with God whispering all the secrets of his thirst in voices overflowing from the depths.

Amir Gilboa

Everyone has a city he calls Jerusalem,
a city he dreams about
until its night-flowers climb the hill
to shed their light on him.
Rising from your dust, Jerusalem,
they light up the evening of his days.

Everyone has a somewhere in Jerusalem
he calls love.
When at the end he comes
barefoot and cold to you,
sweet will be the savor
of your light and soil.

There is a sadness whose name
resembles that of Jerusalem.
When the bells of evening ring,
a last song will descend from your towers
to evoke its name from the stones.

From your dust, Jerusalem,
your night-flowers
will shed their light on him.

Nathan Yonatan

I have loved thee with an everlasting love

Index

Eliane Wilson was born in Switzerland and educated in Lausanne. She is an accomplished anthologist whose talent has found expression in several books published by Shepheard-Walwyn:

Thomas Hardy: An Autobiography in Verse
Edward Thomas: A Mirror of England
Images of Christmas
Oxford: Words & Watercolours

Of the last a reviewer wrote: 'A minor masterpiece. The words and the water-colours do reverberate and go on reverberating like Oxford bells — in an uncanny harmony with one another.'

Eliane Wilson is married to a lawyer. They have two sons and a daughter and live in London.

Mordechai Blum, known to all as Motke, was born in Romania. He emigrated to Palestine in 1944. During this journey, he witnessed the death of his friends when their ship was torpedoed, and he miraculously escaped. For many years, the recurring nightmare accompanied Motke and his canvasses filled with sombre colours, shipwrecked boats and skeletons of ships. Then, anchored in the haven of his beloved Jerusalem, source of his inspiration, and experiencing great happiness in his family life, Motke realised his mystical inner vision, and luminosity and radiance became his palette.

He had moved to Jerusalem in 1951 and at the Bezalel Academy of Arts and Crafts, studied under Mordechai Ardon, Isidor Ashheim, Jacob Steinhardt and the sculptor Ben-Zvi. He also attended a UNESCO-sponsored course on the restoration of mosaics and frescoes given by Professor Orselli, the then Director of the Academy of Fine Arts in Ravenna, gaining a knowledge which he widened during a stay in Ravenna. 'His mosaics,' wrote Ardon, 'have been made, like all mosaics in this country, of the country's stones; but unlike all others, they are far away from mere decorations … they are not superficial, but have depth, in their own mysterious way. Stone seeks stone, stone finds stone, they have been intended for each other from the beginning of time — or so it seems. Mordechai Blum's hands have chosen, selected, and united … their mystery guides and leads the artist's fingers while he works. This is his strength. This power is felt in any work his hands create, whether the result is a mosaic, a collage, or a picture.'

After spending a year in Holland, at the design department of the Royal Factory of Silver Work in Zeist, Motke returned to Jerusalem and opened his studio in 1958. Exhibitions in London, Antwerp and Marseille followed. In the USA his work was exhibited at the Smithsonian Institute, Washington. In South America, at the Museums of Modern Art in Saõ Paulo and Rio de Janeiro. Today Motke is represented in museums and private collections worldwide and the Israel Ministry of Tourism selected two of his paintings to be prestige posters bringing Jerusalem to the world. To the Talmudic words 'Ten measures of beauty were given to the world, and nine of them alighted on Jerusalem,' Motke likes to add Jerusalem gave back to the world ten measures of inspiration of which a spark alighted on him.